Simple Solutions

English Grammar & Writing Mechanics

level 2

Nancy McGraw & Nancy Tondy

Bright Ideas Press, LLC
Cleveland, Ohio

Simple Solutions *level 2*
Grammar & Writing

Printed in the United States of America

ISBN: 0-9772584-2-4

Cover Design: Tim Naujoks
Editor: Kimberly A. Dambrogio, NBCT

Simple Solutions

Note to the Student:

Hello,

This year you will learn many new and exciting things in English, like how to write a good sentence. You will also learn how to use those sentences to write stories. This book will help you practice all of those new things every day so you don't forget them.

Doing the pages in this book every night will help you to become a good writer.

We know you are going to like using this book. We hope you have a really fun year!

Lesson #1

1. Circle the word that rhymes with *rake*.

   farm   bat   cake

2. The **first word in a sentence** has a **capital letter**. Write a word on the line to make the sentence correct.

   (She / she) likes cats.   _____

   (i / I) swam in the pond.   _____

3. Say the word. Fill in the **short** vowel sound.

   f _ _ n   b _ _ t

4. **A sentence tells a complete thought.**

   A sentence tells a ___ thought.

   _____

   -

   _____

5.   Draw lines to match the groups of words to make sentences.

   The ball   goes fast.

   A train   played.

   The boy   rolled away.

6.   Circle the word from the box that belongs with this group.

   dog   cat   bird

   | tree   bag   fish |

7 – 8.   Say each picture name. Write the letter that stands for the **beginning** sound.

Lesson #2

1.   **A sentence tells a complete thought. It starts with a capital letter.**

A sentence tells a complete thought. It starts with

_____

-   letter.

_____

2.   **At the end of a word, "y" almost always says long "e."** Use each word in the correct sentence.

Example: happy   story

_____

- -

She will be _____ to see you.

_____

- -

Tom wrote a funny _____ .

3.   Circle the word that makes the sentence correct.

_____ baked a cake for me.

mom   Mom

4.   Circle the word that rhymes with *bat*.

late   cat   cake

5.   Circle the sentence that tells about the picture.

Max hits the ball.

Max kicks the ball.

6.   Say the picture name. Print the capital and small letters for the **ending** sound.

   _____      _____

7.   Say the picture name. Write the **short** vowel sound on the line.

   _____      _____

8.   Underline the word that names the picture.

rocks   locks   socks

Lesson #3

1.   Draw lines to match the groups of words to make sentences.

My cat   plays all day.

The balloon   popped.

The girl   is furry.

2.   Circle the word from the box that belongs with this group.

red   yellow   blue

bird	sun	green

3.   Circle the word that makes the sentence correct.

_____ like to read.

I   i

4.   Write the word that rhymes with *top*.

_____

cap   mop   box   _____

5.   Say each picture name. Write the consonant letter that stands for the **middle** sound.

ca___el   bea___er

6.   Circle the sentence that tells about the picture.

The girl slides.

The girl swings.

The girl jumps.

7.   Say the word. Fill in the **short** vowel sound.

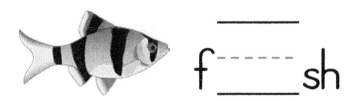

f____sh

8.   Choose a word to make the sentence correct.

Look at the _____ flower.

sunny   pretty

Lesson #4

1. Say the picture name. Write the letters that stand for the **first** and **last** sounds.

___ige___

___obi___

2. Say the picture name. Write the **short** vowel sound.

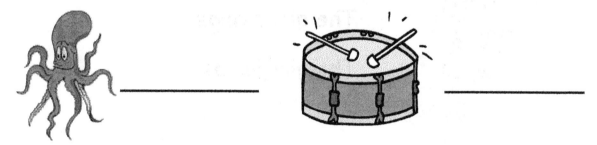

_____   _____

3. Circle the word that rhymes with *net*.

        nest   tent   pet

4. Underline the word that completes the sentence.

    It is fun to sail a _____.

            bone   boat

5.   Every sentence begins with a capital letter.

_____

- - - - - - - - - - - - - - - - - - - -

Every sentence _____ with a

capital letter.

6.   Draw lines to match the groups of words to make sentences.

Mom   is hot.

The sun   drives to school.

The wagon   is full.

7.   Write the word that makes the sentence correct.

_____ has a new bike.

Sue   sue

8.   Which are things to eat?

bus   cake   meat   lake   ham   coat

Lesson #5

1. **The naming part of a sentence tells who or what did or does something.**

   The naming part of a sentence tells who or what

   _____ or _____ something.

2. Write the naming part of the sentence.

   The ball rolled away.

   _____

   -

   What rolled away?   _____

3 – 4.   Say the picture name. Color the pictures that have a **long** vowel sound.

5.   Circle the sentence that tells about the picture.

The boys play cards.

The boys play ball.

The boys ride a bike.

6.   Circle the word that rhymes with *team.*

ten   dream   weed

7.   Which live on a farm?

tiger   bus   cow   lion   hen   desk

8.   Write the letters that stand for the **ending** sound.

 ow____    bucke__

Lesson #6

1. Every sentence begins with a _____ letter.

    capital   small

2. Write the naming part of the sentence.

    The fence was tall.

    _____

    What was tall? -

    _____

3. Underline the word that completes the sentence.

    The mice _____ in the wall.

    hid   fun

4. Write the word that makes this sentence correct.

    _____ sun was very hot.

    The   the

5.   Circle the words that have the same vowel sound.

cot   bat   top   pie   robe   mop

6.   **A sentence tells a complete thought.**

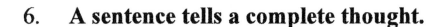

A sentence tells a _____

thought.

7.   **At the end of a word, "y" sometimes says long "i."** Use each word in the correct sentence.

Example: sky   cry

I _____ when I am sad.

The _____ was blue.

8.   Underline the word that names the picture.

fish   fox   frog

Lesson #7

1.   Circle the word that rhymes with *bunny*.

funny   happy   fry

2.   Say the name of the picture. Circle **L** if the vowel is **long** and **S** if the vowel is **short**.

S   L   S   L   S   L

3.   Write the naming part of the sentence.

The pig rolled in the mud.

_____

What rolled in the mud? -

_____

4.   Which are things to wear?

cap   horn   tie   rain   coat   fork

5.   Which word makes the sentence correct?

_____ house is big.

our   Our

6.   Which word has a mistake in it?

mak   late   hide

7.   Spell the word in #6 correctly.

_____

- -

_____

8.   Circle the sentence that tells about the picture.

Ben swims in the lake.

Ben is clean.

Ben plays in the mud.

Lesson #8

1.   Underline the naming part of the sentence.

      The band played a song.

2.   Which are in the sky?

      car   moon   bike   star   jeep   sun

3.   Say the picture name. Write the long vowel sound.

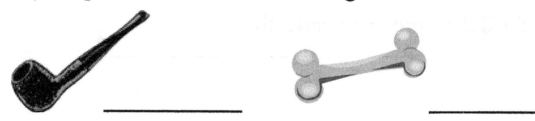

      _____   _____

4.   Which word makes the sentence correct?

      _____ brush is new.

            her   Her

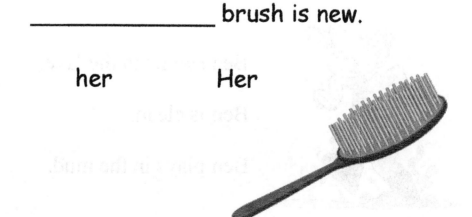

5.   Every sentence begins with a _____ letter.

            capital   small

6.   Write the letter that stands for the middle sound.

      ro___ot   sho___el

7.   Which word has a mistake in it?

                two   four   fiv

8.   Spell the word in #7 correctly.

      _____

      -

      _____

Lesson #9

1. A sentence tells a complete thought.

   True   False

2. Underline the sentence that is correct.

   Ken likes baseball.

   ken likes baseball.

3. Underline the word that rhymes with *goat.*

   bow   clock   coat

4. Draw lines to match the groups of words to make sentences.

   The bird   works here.

   My dad   is a kitten.

   Her pet   hopped in the yard.

5.   Write one of the sentences you made in #4.

_____

- -

_____

_____

- -

_____

6.   Use each word in the correct sentence.

      funny   pretty

      The clown was very _____.

      Anna has a _____coat.

7.   Underline the naming part in the sentence.

      Horses can run fast.

8.   Circle the word in the box that belongs to the group.

      ┌─────────────────────┐
      │ candy   meat   │   orange   apple   grape
      │   peach   │
      └─────────────────────┘

Lesson #10

1. **The action part of a sentence tells what the naming part did or does.**

    Tim watches football.   What does Tim do?

    _____

    -

    _____

2. Every sentence begins with a _____ letter.

    capital   small

3. Say the picture name. Write the letters that stand for the **first** and **last** sounds.

    __abi__

    __izar___

4. Circle the word that rhymes with *hive*.

    sign   five   save

5.   Underline the naming part of the sentence.

The leaf fell from the tree.

6.   Now underline the action part of the same sentence.
      What did the leaf do?

The leaf fell from the tree.

7.   Circle the sentence that tells about the picture.

The children play in the leaves.

The children ride the bus.

The children walk on a log.

8.   Circle the word that has a mistake. Spell the word correctly
      on the line.

after   com   back

_____

_ _ _ _ _ _ _ _ _ _ _ _ _ _ _ _ _

_____

Lesson #11

1.   Underline the sentence that is correct.

we ride the bus to school.

We ride the bus to school.

For #2 and #3 choose an action part
from the Word Box to make a sentence.

| hops |
| was fast |
| saw a spider |
| cried |

_____

2.   **My brother** _____ .

_____

3.   **The bunny** _____ .

4.   Say the picture name. Write the vowel sound you hear.

_____   _____

5.   Underline the naming part of the sentence.

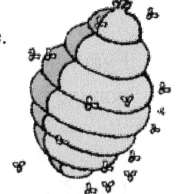

The bees made a hive.

6.   Which are things to ride?

bus   star   horse   lake   bike   train

7.   **A complete sentence has <u>two</u> parts, a <u>naming part</u> and an <u>action part</u>.**

             N   **A**
    Example: The green frog / hopped away.

Write an **N** over the **naming part** of the sentence. Write an **A** over the **action part**.

The two teams had a race.

8.   Say the name of the picture. Circle **L** if the vowel is long and **S** if the vowel is short.

S   L   S   L

Lesson #12

1. Every sentence has _____ parts, a naming part and an action part.

2. Underline the sentence that is correct.

     It rained all day.

     it rained all day.

3. Which word has a mistake in it?

     grow   geos   any

4. Spell the word correctly in #3.

     _____

     -

     _____

5. Underline the naming part of the sentence.

     The bear lives in a cave.

Choose a naming part from the Word Box to begin each sentence.

| Turtles | A man | Chipmunks | She |

6. _____run fast.

7. _____plays music.

8. _____are slow.

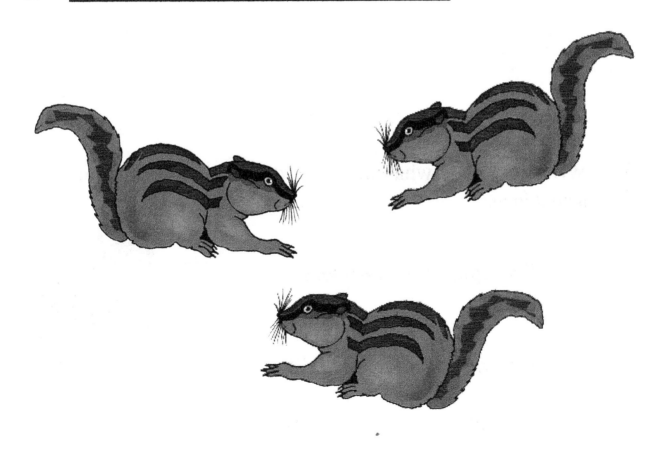

Lesson #13

1. Every sentence has two parts, a naming part and

    an _____ part.

    capital   action

2. Say the name of the picture. Color the pictures that have a
    short vowel sound.

3. Write an **A** over what the spider did. This is the action part of
    a sentence.

    The spider made a web.

4. Circle the word that rhymes with *mail*.

    bait   rain   snail

5.   Read each word group. Underline the complete sentence.
     (Hint: A sentence has <u>both</u> a naming part and an action part.)

     Swims all day.

     The monkey eats bananas.

6.   Add a naming part to the group of
     words in #5 to make it a sentence.

     _____

     -

     _____ swims all day.

7.   When "y" comes at the end of a word it can say long

     "e" or long _____.   ("o" / "i")

8.   Write the letter that stands for the middle sound.

     ra__or   sa__ad

Lesson #14

1.   **A telling sentence tells something. It ends with a period.**

      Example: It is fun to read.

      A telling sentence ends with a _____.

2.   Write a telling sentence of your own.

      It is fun to _____.

3.   Underline the complete sentence.
      (Look for the group that has a
      naming part and an action part.)

      The bird lives in a cage.

      Rides her bike.

4.   Every sentence begins with a _____ letter.

        capital   small

5.   Which are animals?

house   kitten   horse   pig   leaf

6.   Underline the sentence that tells about the picture.

Todd is sad.

Todd rolls on the ground.

Todd laughs.

7.   Put an **A** over the **action part** of this sentence.
      (What did Tia do?)

Tia passed her math test.

8.   Which word has a mistake in it? Write the word correctly.

done   hard   gril

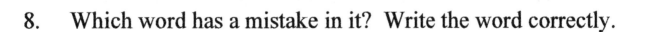

Lesson #15

1. **A telling sentence tells something. It ends with a period. (.)**
   Add a period to this telling sentence to make the sentence
   correct.

   My father is a firefighter___

   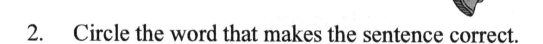

2. Circle the word that makes the sentence correct.

   _____ took a trip to the zoo.

   we   We

3. Underline the action part of the sentence.

   My sister fed our hamster.

4. Match a **naming part** with an **action part** to make a
   sentence. Be sure to add a period to your sentences.

   Three puppies   drives a truck___

   Her bike   played by the pool___

   Uncle Dan   needs new tires___

5.   Underline the word that rhymes with *rose*.

   move   float   nose

6.   Write the letter that stands for the middle sound.

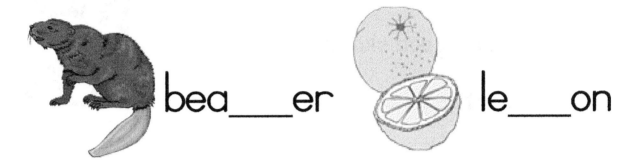

bea___er   le___on

7.   Write a telling sentence. Remember to add a period.

   _____

   -

   My dad is _____

8.   Which words have the same vowel sound?

   tan   team   queen   lawn   seat   bet

Lesson #16

1. Every sentence has _____ parts, a naming part and an action part.

2. Underline the telling sentence that is correct.

    I am a good skater.

    I hate snakes

3. Rewrite the other sentence in #2 to make it correct.

    _____

    -

    _____

4. Underline the action part of this sentence.

    The little squirrel ate a seed.

5. **A question is a sentence that asks something. It ends with a question mark. (?)**

     Example: Do you like school?

     Put a question mark after each question.

     Where are your friends____

     Does your mom work____

6. Which word has a mistake in it?

              some   huose   them

7. Write the correct spelling of the word in #6 on the line.

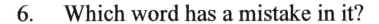

8. Which can fly?

     plane   truck   bird   kite   log

Lesson #17

1. Every sentence begins with a capital letter.

    true   false

2. Add the correct mark to the end of each sentence.

    Can you spell my name____

    Her uncle broke his leg____

    Where do you live____

3. Underline the naming part of the sentence.

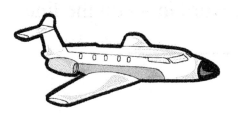

    A pilot flies an airplane.

4. Say each picture name. Write the letter that stands for the beginning sound.

 _____    _____

5.   Read each word group. Underline the complete sentence.

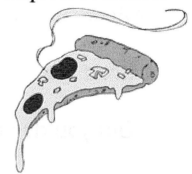

Sarah had a part in the play.

Likes to eat pizza.

6.   Which part of the other sentence in #5 is missing?

naming   action

7.   Write a question below. Don't forget the question mark.

_____

- -

_____

- -

_____

8.   Underline the sentence that tells about the picture.

The boys play a game.

The boys eat a snack.

The boys try to hide.

Lesson #18

1.   After each sentence write **T** for **telling** or **Q** for **question**.

   Brad likes to dive into the pool. _____

   Did you do your homework? _____

   Tara plays the drums. _____

2.   Which part of the sentence is underlined?

   The birds <u>built a nest</u>.

   naming part   action part

3.   Circle the word that rhymes with *brown*.

   best   throw   crown

4.   A sentence tells a complete thought.

   true   false

5. Circle **L** if the vowel sound is **long** and **S** if it is **short**.

S   L   S   L

6. Underline the sentence that is correct.

carl and i ran in a race.

Carl and I ran in a race.

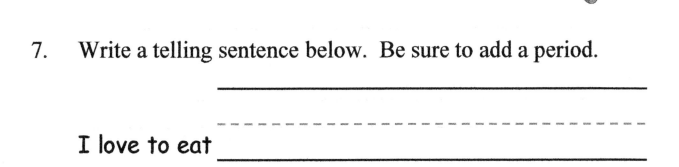

7. Write a telling sentence below. Be sure to add a period.

_____

I love to eat _____

8. Circle the word that has a mistake in it.

two   thre   four

Lesson #19

1. Every question ends with a _____

   A telling sentence ends with a _____

2. Underline the complete sentence.

   Our cub scout troop went fishing.

   My parents.

3. Add some words to the one you didn't underline in #2 to make it a sentence.

   _____

   -

   _____

   _____

   -

   _____

4. Every sentence has a _____ part and an action part.

   naming   question

5.   Put in the correct end mark for each sentence.

       My pants are too short___

       Where is your house___

       How many legs does a spider have___

6.   **An exclamation shows strong feeling like surprise or fear. It ends with an exclamation point. (!)**

       Example: There it is!

    Add an exclamation point to each sentence.

       Look out___

       Wow, what a great idea___

7.   Circle the word that rhymes with *street*.

       feet   strong   swing

8.   Underline the naming part of the sentence. (Who or what made a puddle?)

       The rain made a puddle in our yard.

Lesson #20

1. **An exclamation shows strong feeling like surprise or fear. It ends with an exclamation point. (!)**
    Put in the correct end mark.

    Help me____

    Look at the fire____

2. Which part of the sentence is underlined?

    <u>The stars</u> shine in the sky.

    action part   naming part

3. Rewrite the sentence correctly.
    (There are 2 mistakes.)

    we made a castle

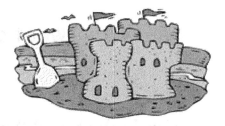

    _____

    -

    _____

4. Which words have the same vowel sound?

    cup   pat   pup   tin   tent   supper

5.   Every sentence begins with a _____ letter.

capital   small

6 – 7.   Match the groups of words to make sentences. Write one
of your sentences on the lines below. Put in an end mark.

Two deer   had a flat tire

The old bike   hid in the woods

_____

- -

_____

_____

- -

_____

8.   Circle the word that belongs to the
group in the box.

| shirt   shoes   socks |

pizza   feet   shorts

Lesson #21

1.   Put in the correct end mark for each sentence.

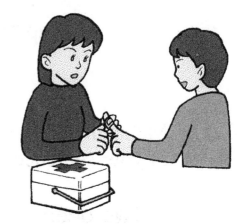

Are you lost___

I hurt my finger___

Watch out___

2.   Underline the action part of this sentence.

Emma lost her mittens.

3.   Which word makes the sentence correct?

_____ read me a bedtime story.

Dad   dad

4.   Circle the word that rhymes with *rope*.

hope   stop   pop

5.   Write your own question. Be sure to put in an end mark.

_____

Do you   _____

_____

6.   Color the pictures that have a long vowel sound.

7.   **A command tells a person to do something. It ends with a period.**   **Example:** Close your eyes.

Put the correct end mark in the commands below.

Be quiet____

Put your paper on my desk____

8.   When "y" comes at the end of a word it can say long

"i" or long _____.   ("e" / "u")

Lesson #22

1. After each sentence write **T** for **telling** or **Q** for **question**.

    Can we go to the movies____

    That truck is huge____

    It was a hot day____

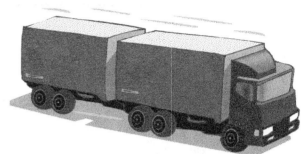

2. Write the sentence correctly. (There are 2 mistakes.)

    she walked home

    _____

    -

    _____

3. Underline the naming part of this sentence.

    The children love to paint.

4. Circle the word that has a
    long vowel sound.

    band   bump   make

5.   Which part of the sentence is underlined?

Megan <u>ate some popcorn</u>.

action part   naming part

6.   True or False: **A command tells someone to do something. It ends with a period.**

true   false

7.   Which word has a mistake in it?

pick   scool   were

8.   Write the correct spelling of the word in #7.

_____

_____

Lesson #23

1. Put in the correct end mark for each sentence.

   Look out___

   Put your clothes away__

   What is your kitten's name__

2. Every sentence _____ with a capital letter.

   begins   ends

3. Match the groups of words to make sentences.

   Fruit   ate the cheese.

   The mouse   is a healthy snack.

4. Write one of the sentences you made below. Be sure to begin
   with a capital letter and to put in an end mark.

   _____

   -

   _____

   _____

   -

   _____

5.   Read each word group. Underline the complete sentence.

   The rainbow.   **Marcus fed his hamster.**

6.   Write the letter that stands for the ending sound.

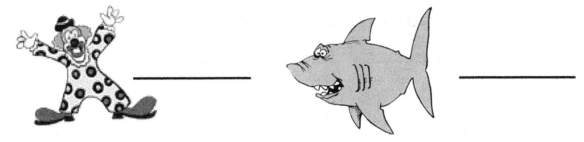

7 – 8.   **The first step in learning to write is to plan what you
      want to say. Sometimes it helps to put your ideas in a
      word web. This is called Prewriting.** Fill in some things
      you like to do after school.

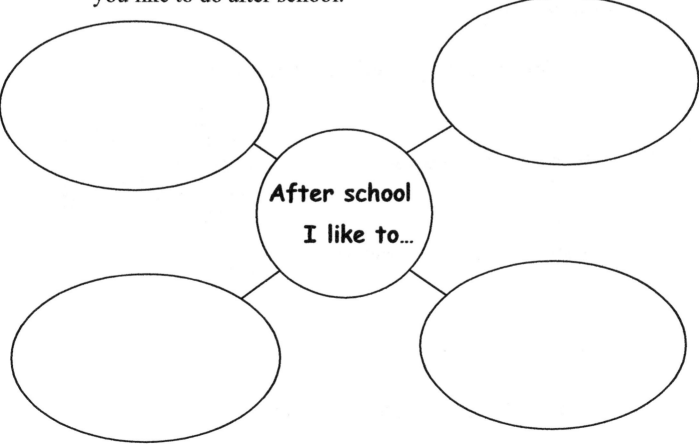

Lesson #24

1. **Every time you use the word *I* in a sentence, write it with a capital letter.**

    Example: I know I am good at baseball.

    Rewrite the sentence using a capital letter for *I*.

    Can i go with you?

    _____

    -

    _____

2. Write an **N** over the **naming** part of the sentence and an **A** over the **action** part.

    My parents played cards with us.

3. Which word rhymes with *green*?

    pen   rain   mean

4. Fill in the correct end mark.

    Put the dishes on the table___

5.   Underline the sentence that is correct.

Wears red boots.

Ryan has a messy desk.

6 – 7.   To help you begin to write, fill in the chart below. List 3 kinds of pets you would like to have and write a name for each one

Kind of Pet	Name

8.   Circle the word that makes the sentence correct.

_____ can jump high.

grasshoppers   Grasshoppers

Lesson #25

1. Circle the sentence that shows the correct use of the word *I*.

   i had fun at the zoo and i want to go back.

   I want to see the bears before I leave.

2. **Whenever you write someone's name or a pet's name, use a capital letter for the first and last name.**

   Example: Maria   Jake   Mike Thomas

   Write the names correctly. Be sure to use a capital letter.

   sue archer _____

   lauren _____

3. What kind of sentence shows strong feeling, like surprise or fear?

   command   exclamation   question

4. Circle the word that has a short vowel sound.

   green   coat   little

5.   Underline the action part of the sentence.

His cat climbed the tree.

6.   After each word group, write *yes* if the word group is a sentence and *no* if it is not a sentence.

Lives in a fishbowl. _____

Pat made a cherry pie. _____

Sat on the swing. _____

7.   Fill in the correct end mark.

Does your sister work here____

8.   Which word has a mistake in it? Write the word correctly on the line.

with   what   whan

_____

_____

Lesson #26

1. Write the names correctly. Be sure to use a capital letter.

    marcus _____

    mary dunn _____

2. Fill in the correct end mark.

    Kyle rode his scooter___

    When do you eat dinner___

3. Which part of the sentence is underlined?

Spiders eat other insects.

action part   naming part

4. Underline the correct sentence.

    Mike and i are best friends.

    I will call you when I can.

5.   Every sentence begins with a _____ letter.

        capital   small

6.   Circle the word that rhymes with *frog*.

        snow   log   big

7 – 8.   To help you get ready to write, fill in the chart with your
         favorite sports.

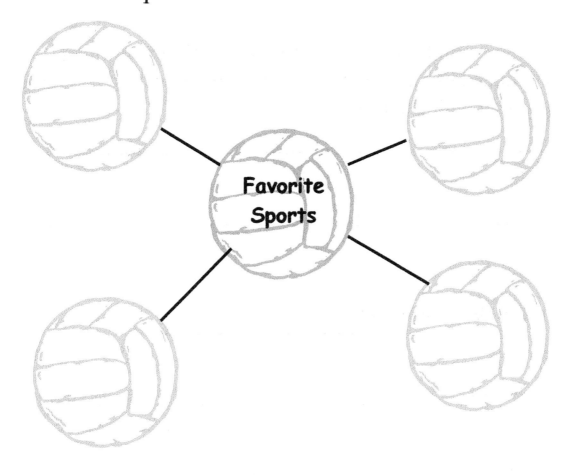

Lesson #27

1.   Underline the naming part of the sentence.

       Ling likes to draw.

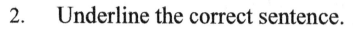

2.   Underline the correct sentence.

       i like trees in the fall?

       Do you have a pet turtle?

3.   A command tells someone to do something. Write a command of your own. Be sure to begin with a capital letter and end with a period.

     _____

     -

     _____

4.   Write the names correctly.

         _____

         - - - - - - - - - - - - - - - - - -

  jason   _____

         _____

         - - - - - - - - - - - - - - - - - -

  cheryl   _____

5.   A telling sentence ends with a period.

         true   false

6.   **Always write days of the week and months of the year with a capital letter.**

     Example: Sunday   April

     Write each day or month with a capital letter.

     march   _____

     tuesday   _____

7.   Which words have the same vowel sound?

     leaf   bread   fire   free   team

8.   Fill in the correct end mark.

     Wow, what a catch____

Lesson #28

1.   Rewrite the sentence correctly. (There are 2 mistakes.)

did you hear the thunder

_____

- -

_____
_____

- -

_____

2.   Fill in the correct end mark.

What time do you go to bed___

Look out___

Raise your hand before you talk___

3.   Write **N** over the **naming** part of the sentence and **A** over the
action part.

Carlos watered the flowers.

4.   Which are insects?

ant   frog   bee   mouse   spider

5. Write each day or month with a capital letter.

    monday _____

    june _____

6. Which word has a mistake in it? Write the word correctly
    on the line.

    read   deos   right _____

7. Underline the correct sentence.

    i like to sleep late on saturdays.

    My mom and I baked bread on Sunday.

8. To help you get ready to write, list your two favorite subjects
    in school.

    _____ and _____

Lesson #29

1. Which part of the sentence is underlined?

    Peter <u>tied his shoes</u>.

    naming part   action part

2. Put in the correct end mark.   Watch out___

3. Circle **L** if the vowel sound is **long** and **S** if the vowel sound is **short**.

    S   L   S   L

4. **Always write holidays using a capital letter.**

    Example: Christmas   Labor Day

    Write the name of the holiday using a capital letter.

    thanksgiving _____

5.   Every sentence has a naming part and an _____ part.

capital   action

6.   Finish the sentence. Make sure to put in an end mark.

_____

Molly cleaned _____

7.   Circle the word that rhymes with *light*.

fight   city   ride

8.   After each word group, write *yes* if the word group is a sentence and *no* if it is not a sentence.

James forgot his homework. _____

Parked the car. _____

I love cherry pie. _____

Jumped rope. _____

Lesson #30

1. Put in the correct end mark.

    Were you stung by the bee____

    Our dog sleeps in the barn____

    Run for your life____

2. Underline the correct sentence.

    I play tennis on Tuesday.

    i play tennis on tuesday.

3. A telling sentence ends with a period.

    true   false

4. Circle the holiday that is written correctly.

    Halloween   easter   labor day

5.   Underline the naming part of the sentence.

The baby deer jumped over the fence.

6.   Write the word correctly.

friday   _____

7 – 8.   Use the web to list 4 things you might do at your birthday party.

Lesson #31

1. **Sometimes you see a word that should begin with a capital letter and it doesn't. We put this mark (☰) under the words that should have a capital letter.**

    Example: my cat's name is ellie.

    Put the mark that means "make capital" under the letters that should begin with a capital letter. (There are 2 words.)

    mark and i are on the same team.

2. Underline the group of words that have both a naming part and an action part.

    Had a great time.

    The ladybug flew in the window.

3. Which word has a mistake in it? Write the correct spelling on the line.

    downe   here   care

    _____

    _____

4. Circle the word that is <u>not</u> written correctly.

    Michael   thanksgiving   Wednesday

5. Which words have a long vowel sound?

    bug   train   fun   spider   cabin

6. Put in the correct end mark.

    Tie your shoes___

    Watch out___

    Do you have a soccer game today___

7. Telling sentences and commands end with a _____.

    question mark   exclamation mark   period

8. Write a command. Be sure to begin with a capital letter and
    end with a period.

    _____

    -

    _____

Lesson #32

1. Use the mark that means "make capital" under the letters that should begin with a capital letter.

    Her name is nancy brown.

2. Which part of the sentence is underlined?

    David <u>built a birdhouse</u>.

    naming part   action part

3. Fill in the correct end mark.

    Which girl has the longest hair____

4. Which holiday is written incorrectly? Write it correctly on the line.

    christmas   Earth Day   Columbus Day

    _____

    -

    _____

5.   Circle the word that rhymes with *wish*.

          with   dish   fifth

6.   After each word group, write **yes** if the word group is a
     sentence and **no** if it is not a sentence.

     Live in the ocean. _____

     Jesse fed the lamb. _____

     Her blue coat. _____

7.   Every sentence begins with a _____ letter.

          capital   small

8.   Look at the picture. Pretend this is
     your tree house. List 2 things you
     might do in your tree house.

     1) _____

     2) _____

Lesson #33

1. **Sometimes a title is used before a person's name. A title begins with a capital letter and usually ends with a period.**

   Example: Mrs. Lane   Mr. Rogers   Miss Smith

   Write each title correctly.

   mr. Davis _____

   mrs. Pike _____

2. Underline the correct sentence.

   Yesterday I fell off of my bike.

   Marcus and i are brothers.

3. Underline the action part of the sentence.

   My puppy buried his bone.

4. Write the word correctly.

   monday _____

5.   Every sentence has _____ parts, a naming part
      and an action part.

6.   Add the correct end mark to this exclamation.

      Wow, what a scary movie____

7.   Which word has a mistake? Write
      the word correctly on the line.

         three   famaly   long

      _____

8.   Which word makes the sentence correct?

      _____ come out at night.

              Owls   owls

Lesson #34

1. **Sometimes a title is used before a person's name. A title begins with a capital letter and often ends with a period.**
    Write each title correctly.

    miss Jackson _____

    mr. Dennis _____

2. Circle the words with the same vowel sound.

    fox   goat   cot   told   sock

3. Underline the naming part of the sentence.

    Greg and I play the piano.

4. Use capital letters correctly.

    sunday _____

    mothers day _____

5.   Use the marks to show which words should begin with a capital letter. (☰)

i had basketball practice over christmas break.

6.   Write the letter that stands for the middle sound.

spi___er   ca___e

7.   Every holiday is written with a capital letter.

true   false

8.   Add an <u>action part</u> to this group of words to make a sentence. Be sure to add a period at the end of your sentence.

The little fox _____

Lesson #35

1.   Fill in the correct end mark.

   Where did you put your coat_____

   Pick up your toys _____

2.   Underline the correct sentence.

      miss James is my teacher.

      My neighbor is Mrs. Morrow.

3 – 4.   Use the circle to help you plan what to write. List one
         thing you like to do in each season.

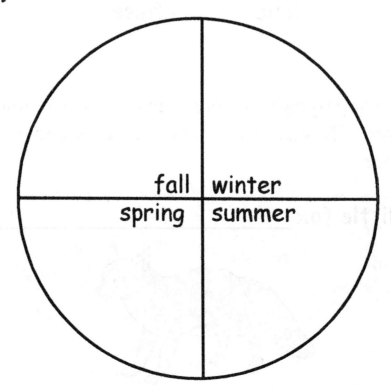

fall | winter

spring | summer

5.   Which part of the sentence is underlined?

The <u>children</u> saw a crab on the sand.

action part   naming part

6.   Write the mark that means "make capital."

_____

7.   Circle the word that rhymes with *cry*.

day   dry   time

8.   Finish the question below. Be sure
       to put in the correct end mark.

Did you _____

Lesson #36

1. Underline the group of words that have both a naming part and an action part.

   The rocket.

   The house was cold last night.

2. **Sometimes you forget to put a period at the end of your sentence. We use the mark (⊙) to show "add a period."**

   Example: I tied a knot in the rope⊙

   Add this mark (⊙) in the sentence below.

   Last night for dinner we had bean soup

3. Write the word correctly.

   saturday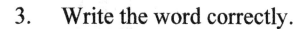

4. Fill in the correct end mark.

   Yea, we won

5.   Circle the word with a long vowel sound.

frog   candy   heat

6.   Every sentence _____ with a capital letter.

begins   ends

7.   Rewrite the sentence correctly.

i had to go to the doctor ⊙

_____

_____

8.   Write the titles correctly.

miss _____

mrs. _____

Lesson #37

1.   Rewrite the sentence correctly.

sometimes i stay up late.

_____

_____

2.   Underline the correct sentence.

Every Thursday I stay after school.

My favorite day is halloween.

3.   Which word has a mistake in it? Write the word correctly
     on the line.

        yelow   brown   black

     _____

4.   Every sentence has a naming part and an _____ part.

              ending   action

5. Fill in the correct end mark.

Have you seen my slippers___

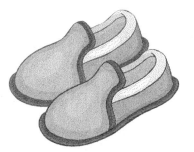

6. Circle the holiday that has a mistake.

thanksgiving   Mother's Day   Earth Day

7. Write the correct end mark after each sentence type.

Exclamation _____

Command _____

Question _____

Telling _____

8. Name your two favorite rides at an amusement park.

A)_____

B)_____

Lesson #38

1. Add the mark ⊙ to show "add a period."

   My aunt took us to the circus

2. Add the correct end mark.

   When did you go to New York____

3. Which are things to wear on your feet?

   scarf   boots   mittens   slippers   ring

4. Write the titles correctly.

   mr. _____

   miss _____

5. Days of the week and months of the year are always written with a capital letter.

   true   false

6 – 7.   You found a bag of money. What do you buy with it?

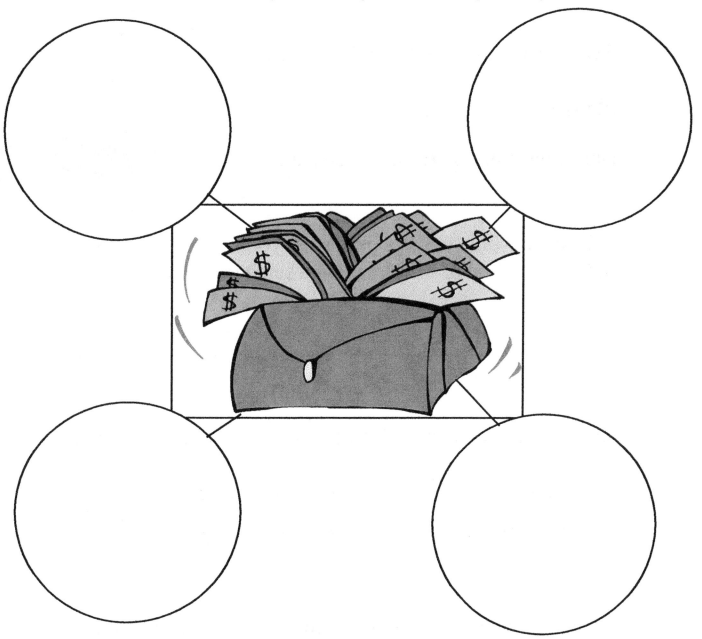

8.   Put an **N** above the **naming** part of the sentence and an **A** above the **action** part.

My cousins came for the weekend.

Lesson #39

1. Read each word group. Underline the complete sentence.

    Planted the flowers.

    Grandma bakes the best cookies.

2. Add some words to the word group you
    didn't underline in #1 to make it a sentence.

    _____

3. Match a naming part with an action part to make a sentence.

    The rabbit   won the race.

    Our team   hopped away.

4. Write one of the sentences you made in #3. Be sure to begin
    with a capital letter and end with a period.

    _____

    _____

5.   Write the mark that means "make capital."

_____

6.   Which word has a spelling mistake?

clock   pond   dor

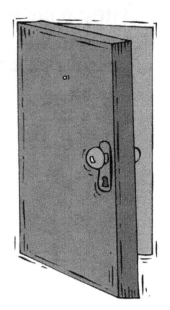

7.   Rewrite the sentence correctly.

our garden has beans

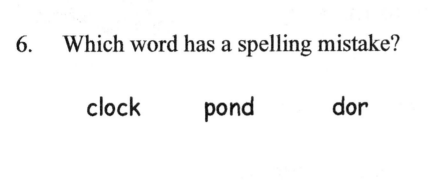

_____

_____

8.   The naming part of a sentence tells what
      someone or something did or does.

true   false

Lesson #40

1.   Fill in the correct end mark.

They painted their house white___

Yea, we're going to the fair__

2.   Underline the action part of the sentence.

Mason walked under the ladder.

3.   Which word has a short vowel sound?

skate   free   dish

4.   Underline the correct sentence.

Rita goes horseback riding on saturdays.

Every Monday we go out to dinner.

5. Use the marks that mean "make capital" and "add a period" to fix this sentence. (There are 3 mistakes.)

eva and i live next door to each other

6. What kinds of words should begin with a capital letter?

holidays   days of the week   titles   all of these

7. **A compound word is made when two words are put together to make a new word.**

    Example: lady + bug ➡ ladybug
    bed + time ➡ bedtime

    Put the words together to make a new word.

day + time ➡ _____

8. Which word has a spelling mistake?

best   babi   begin

Lesson #41

1. After each word group, write *yes* if the word group is a sentence and *no* if it is not a sentence.

    Our family went on a picnic. _____

    Laughed at the joke. _____

2. Use capital letters correctly.

    mr. - _____

    wednesday - _____

    thanksgiving - _____

3. Which part of the sentence is underlined?

    Taylor <u>cooked hotdogs on the grill</u>.

    naming part   action part

4. Circle the words that have the same vowel sound.

    hot   door   knot   box   out

5. A compound word is made when two words are put together to make a new word. Put the words together to make a new word.

    base + ball ➡ _____

    bath + room ➡ _____

6. **A word that names a person is called a noun.**

    Example: My <u>mother</u> is a <u>teacher</u>.
                   The <u>baby</u> laughed.

    Underline the word that names a person.

    My grandma served cake.

7 – 8. Write a telling sentence below. Be sure to begin with a capital letter and to put in an end mark.

    _____

    _____

    _____

Lesson #42

1. Underline the two main parts of every sentence.

    compound   action   naming   command

2. Put in the correct end mark.

    Where did you get that idea___

    Watch out___

3. Rewrite the sentence correctly.

    <u>m</u>ia brushed her dog, <u>f</u>luffy⊙

    _____

    _____

4. Which word rhymes with *small*?

    large   tell   fall

5.   Underline the sentence that is correct.

The eagle.

The bird had a broken wing.

6.   **A word that names a person is called a noun.**
Underline the word that names a person.

The boys went on the rollercoaster.

7 – 8.   Your family is taking a trip to the ocean. What will you
see when you get there? List some things on the lines.

_____   _____

_____   _____

Lesson #43

1.   Make a compound word by putting the two words together.

     fast + ball ➡ _____

     paint + brush ➡ _____

2.   **A noun can also name a place.**

     Example: Hank went to the <u>lake</u>.
                          We have recess at <u>school</u>.

     Underline the noun that names a place.

     Our family went to the park.

3.   Use capital letters correctly.

     saturday - _____

     april - _____

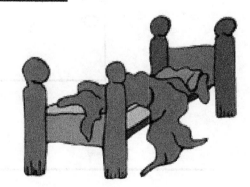

4.   Fill in the correct end mark.

     Make your bed___

5. Write the letter that stands for the ending sound.

rabbi___   tuli___

6. Use the mark that means "make capital" to fix the sentence below. (There are 2 mistakes.)

    i am having my first sleepover on friday.

7. Which word has a spelling mistake?
    Write the word correctly on the line.

    fast   each   beter

    _____

8. Circle the word that makes this sentence correct.

    _____ a picture of a monkey.

    Draw   draw

Lesson #44

1. A **compound word** is two words that are put together to make a new word. Underline the compound word below.

   I have to do my homework as soon as I get home.

2. Write the word correctly.

   tuesday _____

3. **Words that mean about the same thing are called synonyms.** (sĭn-ō-nĭms)

   Example: Large and huge mean the same as big.

   Choose two words from the Word Box that mean about the same thing as *happy*.

sad	cheerful	small	glad

   _____   _____

4. Which word has a long vowel sound?

   water   deep   under

5.   Underline the naming part of this sentence.

Liam plays guitar very well.

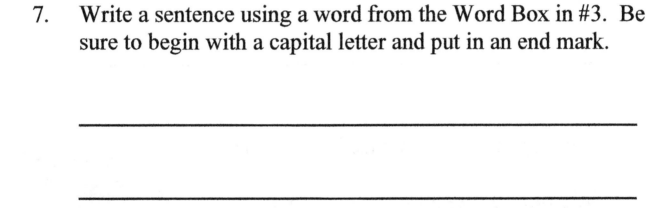

6.   Fill in the correct end mark.

What a great idea___

Shane is the smartest boy in the class___

7.   Write a sentence using a word from the Word Box in #3. Be sure to begin with a capital letter and put in an end mark.

_____

_____

8.   **A noun can also name a place.** Underline the noun that names a place.

We visited my cousins on their farm.

Lesson #45

1 – 2. **After you plan your writing, you can begin to write.
This is called Drafting.** Don't worry if you spell some
words wrong or if you forget to put in an end mark.
You'll be able to fix your mistakes later.

Look back at Lesson #38. Write 2 sentences telling what
you would do if you found a bag of money.

_____

_____

_____

3.   Which part of the sentence is underlined?

<u>We</u> heard a cricket in our yard.

naming part   action part

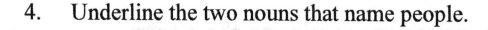

4.   Underline the two nouns that name people.

My sister is a nurse.

5. Use the "make capital" mark to show which words should be capitalized.

    puppy   steve   july   sunday   pie

6. **Words that mean about the same thing are called synonyms.** Choose a word from the box that means about the same thing as each word below.

    | tiny   small   icy   chilly   happy |

    little _____

    cold _____

7. **Sometimes you spell a word with a capital letter and it should begin with a lower case letter. This mark means "make lower case." (/)**
    Example: Sarah baked an Apple pie.

    Find the word in the sentence that should not be written with a capital letter. Use the new mark. (/)

    Her Brother plays golf.

8. Circle the word that rhymes with *pick.*

    stick   pack   pipe

Lesson #46

1.   **Nouns can also name things.**

   Example: Her <u>car</u> is green. *Car* names a thing.

   Underline the word in the sentence that names a thing.

   I dug up a carrot.

2.   Every sentence begins with a ____ letter.

   capital   small

3 – 4.   Use nouns from the word box to finish the sentences.

| house   ladder   pool   ball |

   We jumped into the _____ today. We

took a _____ in the water to play catch.

We used the _____ when it was time

to get out. We went into the

_____ to eat a snack.

5.   Underline the group of words that makes a sentence.

The bike was a big surprise.

Wore a bib.

6 – 7. Go back to Lesson #37. Write two sentences about your
         favorite ride at an amusement park.

My favorite ride is _____

_____

_____

_____

8.   Which word means almost the same
       as *happy*?

   mad   funny   glad

Lesson #47

1. **This is the mark to show "make lower case." (/)**
    Find the word in the sentence that should not be written with
    a capital letter. Use the new mark. (/)

    A Turtle's shell is very hard.

2. Underline the action part of the sentence.

    The fish swam around in the bowl.

3. Underline the nouns that name a place.
    (There are 2.)

    There is a church next to my school.

4. Use capital letters correctly.

    halloween - _____

    december - _____

5.   Fill in the correct end mark.

        Put on your pajamas____

6.   What do these nouns name?

        | carrot   horse   hammer   bike |

        a person   a place   a thing

7.   Write the mark that means "add a period."   _____

8.   Choose a word from the Word Box
      that means almost the same thing as
      the underlined word.

        | close   raced   scream |

      <u>Shut</u> the door. _____

      Don't <u>yell</u> at me. _____

      Amy <u>ran</u> to the store. _____

Lesson #48

1. Underline the nouns that name a person. (There are 2.)

    The teachers played the students in a baseball

    game.

2. Underline the naming part of the sentence.

    Thomas drank a big glass of milk.

3. Add the "make lower case" mark and the "add a period"
    mark to fix this sentence.

    A bee landed on my Lunch

4. Choose a word from the Word Box that means about the
    same thing as each word below.

noisy	jump	thin	below

    hop _____

    loud _____

5.   Nouns can name people, places, or things. (Use the Help
     Pages if you can't remember.)

          true   false

6.   Fill in the correct end mark.

          How tall are you___

          Wow, your turtle is huge___

          Please set the table___

7 – 8. Someone left a gift by your front door. List some things
        that may be inside.

        _____

        _____

        _____

        _____

Lesson #49

1. Rewrite the sentence correctly.

do you and/Your sister like cake?

_____

_____

2. Which word has a short vowel sound?

feet   swim   chain

3. What do you call words that mean almost the same as another word? (Use your Help Pages.)

nouns   synonyms

4. Underline the action part of the sentence.

Hank saved his money to buy a video game.

5. Look back at the last lesson. Write two
    sentences about what was inside the package
    when you opened it. Begin each sentence
    with a capital letter and use end marks.

    _____

    _____

    _____

6. Which word is written correctly?

    Easter   august   wednesday

7. Underline the nouns that name a place.

    school   teacher   park   grocery   kitten

8. Make 2 compound words using
    the words from the box.

sun	bow
light	rain

    _____   _____

Lesson #50

1. Fill in the correct end mark.

    Ouch, that really hurt___

2. Write the two nouns in this sentence.

    The swimmers are at the pool.

    _____

    _____

3. Rewrite the sentence correctly.

    the winners will get a prize

    _____

    _____

4. Circle the word that rhymes with *teach*.

    team   get   beach

5. **Words that mean the opposite of each other are called antonyms.**

    Example: The opposite of <u>fast</u> is <u>slow</u>.
    The opposite of <u>wet</u> is d<u>ry</u>.

    Circle the antonym or opposite of the word.

    easy ➡   close   cold   hard

    tall ➡   drink   short   hot

6. Underline the correct sentence.

    i will call you as soon as i can.

    My dad and I went fishing.

7. Every sentence has _____ parts,
    a naming part and an action part.

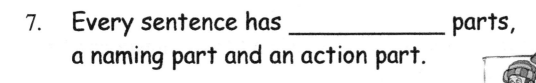

8. Use capital letters correctly.

    sharon _____

    mrs. _____

Lesson #51

1. After each word group, write *yes*
    if the word group is a sentence
    and *no* if it is not a sentence.

    Broke the dish. _____

    I saw a deer in my yard. _____

    My grandpa. _____

2. Circle the <u>antonym</u> or the opposite of the word.

    asleep ➡ awake   tired   dry

    dirty ➡ wet   clean   loud

3. Use the marks for "make capital" and "make lower case" to
    fix the sentence below.

    she is Hungry for a pear.

4. A sentence tells a complete thought.

    true   false

5.   Underline the nouns that name things in this sentence.

I need a pencil, an eraser, and a book bag.

6.   Underline the word that means almost the same as the underlined word.

My mom says I am too <u>thin</u>.

fat   skinny   loud

7.   Write a sentence using a compound word from the box.

everyone   birthday   homework

_____

_____

8.   A command ends with a period.

yes   no

Lesson #52

1.   Which part of the sentence is underlined?

     The boys <u>talked during the movie</u>.

     naming part   action part

2.   Put the "make capital" marks under any words that should begin with a capital letter.

     flag   july   sunday   miss

3.   Circle the synonym for (word that means almost the same as) *pretty*.

     smart   nice   beautiful

4.   Underline the nouns that name people in this sentence. (There are 2.)

     Each of the teams has nine players.

5 – 6. Look back at your writing circle from Lesson #35.
Choose one season and write 2 sentences about what you
like to do during that season.

_____

_____

_____

7. Join the two words to make
a compound word.

water + melon

_____

8. Fill in the correct end mark.

Wow, what a great pie___

Who lost their hat___

My bedroom is blue___

Lesson #53

1.   **Some nouns name special people, places, or things.**
     These are called proper nouns.

     Example: a person or pet's name - Eric or Muffin
                    a special place - Ohio

     Write a special name next to each word below.

     city _____   girl _____

2.   Circle the word that means the opposite of *stand*.

                  slow   sit   heavy

3.   Underline the word group that is a sentence.

     Walked home from school.

     My friend lives in Columbus.

4.   Every sentence begins with a _____ letter.

                  lower case   capital

5.   Which word has a spelling mistake?

        beter   both   begin

6.   Use the mark for "make lower case"
      in this sentence.

      The Birds made a nest in the tree.

7.   Write this sentence correctly.

      Jackie and joan are best friends.

      _____

      _____

8.   Which word means almost the
      same as *pick*?

      awake   choose   yell

Lesson #54

1.   Underline the naming part of the sentence.

Keisha cleaned her room before lunch.

2.   After you do your writing, you need to look at what you wrote to see if you can **make your writing better.** This is the time to **fix spelling mistakes** and **missing end marks.** **This is called Revising.**

Read the sentence below and use the marks for "make capital," "make lower case," and "add a period" to fix the sentence.

At recess i fell down on the Playground

3.   Underline the noun that names a person.

The girls read a poem

in the play.

4.   Make a compound word by joining the words below.

oat + meal ➡ _____

5.   Write the correct end mark after each sentence type.

Exclamation _____

Command   _____

Question   _____

Telling   _____

6.   Some nouns name special people, places, or things. These are called proper nouns.

Example: boy - Todd

Write a proper noun for the word below.

school - _____

7.   Circle the word that has a long vowel sound.

jump   glass   white

8.   Underline the action part of the sentence.

The giraffe ate leaves.

Lesson #55

1. Underline the nouns that name a thing.

    ### The books were under the table.

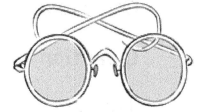

2. Fill in the correct end mark.

    ### Where are your glasses___

3. Fill in the special mark next to each phrase.

    Add a period - _____

    Make a capital - _____

    Make lower case - _____

4. List your three favorite things to eat for dinner.

    _____

    _____

    _____

5.   Nouns can name people, places, or things.

                    true   false

6.   Underline the naming part of the sentence.

       The king lived in a castle.

7.   Use words from the box to make
       two compound words.

| pop | yard | flash | corn | back |

       _____

       _____

8.   Read the sentence below and use the special marks to make
       the sentence better.

            ricky put bugs in a jar

Lesson #56

1. Which word is a synonym for (means almost the same as) the word *bad*?

   small   nice   terrible

2. Underline the proper noun in this sentence. (What word names a special person, place, or thing?)

   Marta put her books in a box.

3. Which word has a spelling mistake?
   Write the correct spelling on the line.

   anything   aruond   behind

   _____

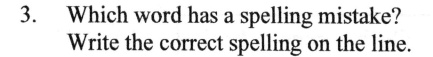

4. Write the sentence correctly by fixing the mistakes.

   my ice cream ꝓropped on the floor⊙

   _____

   _____

5.   Fill in the end mark.

Wow, what an easy test___

6.   Use capital letters correctly.

monday _____

january _____

7.   **Sometimes you write a noun that names more than one. Most times you add an "s" to name more than one.**

Example: boy ➡ boys   desk ➡ desks

Make each noun name more than one.

friend ➡ _____

parent ➡ _____

8.   Which part of the sentence is underlined?

<u>Nick</u> cut the grass.

naming part   action part

Lesson #57

1. **Most times you add an "s" to name more than one.**
    Make each noun name more than one.

    chair ➡ _____

    bird ➡ _____

2. Add the marks for "make capital" and
    "add a period" to fix this sentence.

    tyrone bought popcorn at the movies

3. Which word rhymes with *name*?

    fan   class   flame

4. Use words from the Word Box to make a compound word.

paint	head	brush	light

    _____

5.   Underline the group of words that makes a sentence.

Anna sent me a card.

Went out for dinner.

6.   Underline the proper noun.

We live on Maple Street.

7.   Fill in the end mark.

Stay in your seat__

Boy, my dad was surprised__

Did you finish your math homework__

8.   Underline the noun that names a place.

We drove to the mall.

Lesson #58

1. Use the "make capital" marks to tell which words should begin with a capital letter.

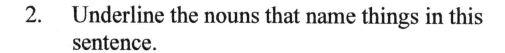

     teacher   april   fall   mr.

2. Underline the nouns that name things in this sentence.

Lee needs a marker, a ruler, and a pencil.

3. Write the word that is a proper noun in #3.

_____

4. Look back at Lesson #23. Write two sentences about what you like to do after you get home from school.

_____

_____

_____

5.   Make a compound word.

wind + mill ➡ _____

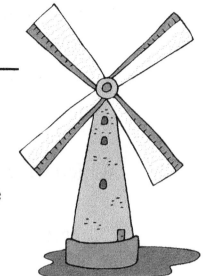

6.   Find the word in the sentence that should
      not be written with a capital letter. Use the
      mark to show "make lower case." (/)

      Henry loves to eat Pancakes.

7.   Which word means the opposite of the word *above*?

          old   quick   below

8.   Rewrite this sentence correctly.

      shelly and I built a snow fort ⊙
      ‗

      _____

      _____

      _____

Lesson #59

1.   Underline the action part of this sentence.

     The monkeys played in their cage.

2.   Which word has a spelling mistake?

     frum   any   along

3.   Spell the word correctly below.

     _____

4.   Fill in the end mark.

     Did you go to the museum___

     Wow, did we have fun___

     Comb your hair___

5.   Make these nouns mean more than one.
     Example: one pencil ➡ <u>two pencils</u>

     one girl ➡ three _____

     one paper ➡ two _____

6.   Underline the proper noun.

     Our team is the Bulldogs.

7.   Use the special marks to fix this sentence. (There are 2 mistakes.)

     I like to run through the Sprinkler

8.   Underline the sentence that is correct.

     Ryan likes books about animals.

     The turkey.

Lesson #60

1.   Underline the noun that names a person.

   The dentist pulled my tooth.

2.   Which word is a synonym for (means almost the same as) the word *make*?

   give   build   giant

3.   Every sentence begins with a _____ letter.

   capital   lower case

4.   Fill in the special mark next to each phrase.

   Add a period _____

   Make a capital _____

   Make lower case _____

5.   Which word has a short vowel sound?

safe   neat   twin

6.   Which part of the sentence is underlined?

<u>Sarah</u> dropped her milk on the floor.

naming part   action part

7.   Use the words in the Word Box to make a compound word.

after   road   noon   rail

_____

8.   Write another compound word from the Word Box.

_____

Lesson #61

1.   Make these nouns mean more than one.

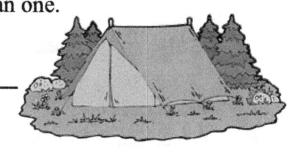

     camp - _____

     mitten - _____

2.   Underline the action part of the sentence.

     Mrs. Jackson passed out our math test.

3.   Fill in the correct end mark.

     Did you break your leg___

     What a great gift___

4.   A telling sentence and a command
     end with what end mark?

     question mark   period   exclamation mark

5.   Add the marks for "make capital" and "make lower case" to
     fix this sentence.

        my sister made a Blueberry pie.

6.   Write the word from the sentence above
     that is a compound word.

     _____

7.   Which word is an antonym of (means the opposite of) the
     word *inside*?

     inside ➡   first   outside   dirty

8.   Read each word group. Underline the group that makes a
     complete thought.

        Mr. Gallo.

        This box is light.

        Ran out of sugar.

Lesson #62

1 – 2. Draw a picture. Write two sentences about your picture.

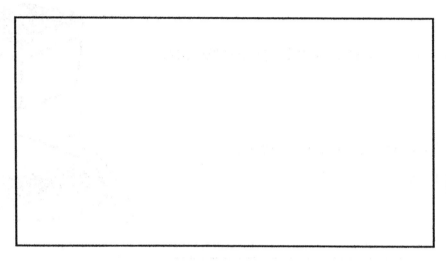

_____

_____

_____

3. Which word has a short vowel sound?

yell   scream   place

4. Fill in the correct end mark.

Hang up your coat____

5.   Underline the sentence that is written correctly.

Sarah and i went for a walk

I take out the trash on Mondays.

6.   **A noun names people, places, and**

_____.

cars   books   things

7.   Make a compound word from the 2 words
     below.

flash + light ➡ _____

8.   Use the compound word from #7 in a sentence.

_____

_____

_____

Lesson #63

1.   Write the mark that means "make lower case." _____

2.   Choose a word from the box that means almost the same thing as (is a synonym for) the underlined word.

angry   tug   below

The cat went <u>under</u> the table. _____

My mom was very <u>mad</u> at me. _____

The puppy tried to <u>pull</u> the rope._____

3.   Which word has a spelling mistake? Write the word correctly on the line.

bring   fathar   been

_____

4.   Underline the naming part of this sentence.

      The wasp stung me on the foot.

5.   Add the marks for "make capital" and "add a period" to show how to fix the sentence below.

      My cousin lives in new york

6.   Circle the proper noun.

      school   store   Jason

7.   The **naming part** of a sentence tells **who** or **what** did something.

      true   false

8.   Fill in the correct end mark.

      How much does a whale weigh___

Lesson #64

1.   Make these nouns mean more than one.

      one bear ➡ five _____

      one wagon ➡ two _____

2.   Underline the group of words that have a naming part and an action part.

      I wrote a note to my grandma.

      Washed the car.

3.   Which word rhymes with *might*?

         late   fight   fire

4.   Rewrite this sentence correctly.

      ben won a trophy ⊙
      =

      _____

5.　**A pronoun takes the place of a noun.**

　　Example:　Maria walks.　➡ <u>She</u> walks.
　　　　　　　　The bus stopped.　➡ <u>It</u> stopped.
　　　　　　　　Hank and Tim play.　➡ <u>They</u> play.

Choose a pronoun from the Word Box to take the place of the underlined words in the sentence.

He	They	She

<u>Steve and Kyle</u> got hurt.　　　_____

<u>Molly</u> had a cold.　　　_____

6.　Fill in the end mark.

　　I drank a whole gallon of milk___

7.　Underline the nouns that name things. (There are 2.)

　　Matt wrote a paper and made a poster.

8.　Circle the proper noun in the sentence above.

Lesson #65

1. Choose a pronoun from the box to take the place of the underlined noun in the sentence.

He	They	She	It

    <u>Clothes</u> are on the floor. _____

    <u>Lynn</u> put the clothes away. _____

    <u>Thomas</u> cleaned the rug. _____

2. Underline the action part of the sentence.

    My family moved to Arizona.

3. Add the marks for "make capital" and "add a period" to show how to fix this sentence.

    gina loves living in the country

4. Which word means almost the same as the word *big*?

    big ➡ small   help   huge

5.   Fill in the correct end mark.

I like to put jelly on my toast___

6.   Put the words together to make a compound word.

drive + way ➡ _____

7.   Circle the nouns that name places.

We drove to the airport and

the drugstore.

8.   Use the compound word from the #6 in a sentence.

_____

_____

_____

Lesson #66

1. Nouns name people, places, and things.

    true   false

2. Use the "make capital" marks to show
    which words should be capitalized.

    mom   saturday   kitten   april

3. After each word group, write **yes** if the word group is a
    sentence and **no** if it is not a sentence.

    Molly broke the bedroom window. _____

    Built a snowman. _____

    He threw a snowball at me. _____

4. Choose one of the compound words in the
    sentences above and use it in a sentence.

    _____

    _____

5. Choose a word from the box that means "the opposite" of each word below.

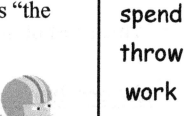

spend
throw
work

play _____

save _____

catch _____

6. Use a pronoun from the box to take the place of the words below.

| he | they | she | it |

my aunt_____

the jet_____

7 – 8. A genie will grant you 3 wishes. What do you wish for?

1)_____

2)_____

3)_____

Lesson #67

1. Which part of the sentence is underlined?

    <u>My brother and I</u> flew our new kite.

    action part   naming part

2. Look at the sentence above. **When you write or talk about another person and yourself, <u>name yourself last</u>. The word "I" will always be used in the naming part of the sentence.**

    Rewrite the sentence below to make it correct.

    Me and Gina rode our bikes.

    _____

3. Every sentence begins with a _____ letter.

        lower case   capital

4. Write the mark that means "add a period."   _____

5.   Circle the nouns in the sentence that name people.
      (There are 2.)

      My coach told the team to work harder.

6.   Make these nouns name more than one.

      one hamster ➡ nine _____

      one goat ➡ four _____

7.   Use capital letters correctly.

      president's day _____

      mrs._____

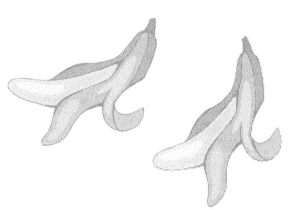

8.   Rewrite the sentence correctly.

      i ate two bananas.

      _____

Lesson #68

1. Fill in the correct end mark.

    What is your favorite color___

    Help, my foot is stuck___

2. Use a pronoun to take the place of the underlined noun. (Use *he*, *she*, *they*, or *it*.)

    <u>Ryan</u> scored a touchdown.   _____

3. Look at sentence #2. Write the compound word in the sentence.

    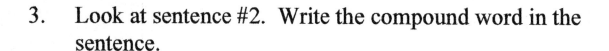

4. Underline the sentence that is written correctly.

    I and Susan won the race.

    Susan and I won the race.

5. Which word is a synonym for the word *neat*? (Use the Help
    Pages if you need to.)

    neat ➡ pretty   tidy   friendly

6. Make these nouns name more than one.

    lion ➡ _____

    kite ➡ _____

7. Underline the nouns that name things.

    I play the drums, the guitar, and the piano.

8. After each sentence, write **T** for **telling**, **C** for **command**, or
    Q for **question**.

    Call your mom. _____

    What is her number? _____

    I will have to look it up. _____

Lesson #69

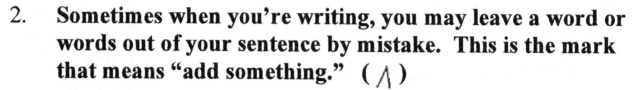

1. Use a pronoun to take the place of the underlined noun. (Use *he*, *she*, *they*, or *it*.)

    <u>Michael</u> learned to play the flute. _____

2. **Sometimes when you're writing, you may leave a word or words out of your sentence by mistake. This is the mark that means "add something." (∧)**

    Example: Mom baked ∧cherry pie.
                        a

    Read this sentence. Use the new mark to show where a word should be added.

    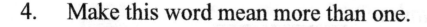

    We went to store.

3. Underline the nouns in the sentence. (There are 2.)

    Her brother works at the gym.

4. Make this word mean more than one.

    one computer ➡ two _____

5. Underline the correct sentence.

    Me and Larry like to sing.

    Larry and I like to sing.

6. Underline the naming part of the sentence.

    Shawna dropped an egg on the floor.

7 – 8. Look back at Lesson #66. What did you wish for from the
genie? Write two or three sentences below.

_____

_____

_____

_____

_____

_____

Lesson #70

1. Which word means almost the same as the word *small*?

    small ➡   nice   tiny   beautiful

2. Fill in the correct end mark.

    Did your dog run away____

    Yea, it's Christmas____

3. Fill in the special mark next to each phrase.

    Add a period - _____

    Make a capital - _____

    Make lower case - _____

    Add something - _____

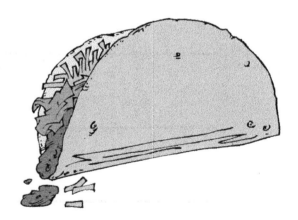

4. Underline the proper noun in this sentence.

    I told Michelle to order the tacos.

5.   Use the mark for "add something" to show where a word should be added.

Our class went ice skating the pond.

6.   Use the Word Box to make 2 compound words.

| brush | eye | paint | lash |

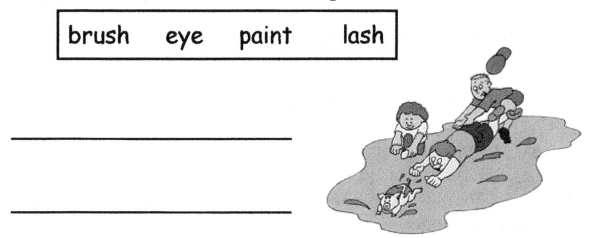

_____

_____

7.   Underline the noun that names people.

Three boys chased the pig.

8.   Fill in an action part to this sentence and write it on the line. Be sure to put in an end mark.

The bird_____

_____

Lesson #71

1. Underline the correct sentence.

   Me and Ming washed the dog.

   Ming and I washed the dog.

2. Which word means the opposite of the word *cheerful*?

   cheerful ➡   happy   sad   angry

3. Use the marks for "make capital" and "add something" to fix this sentence.

   the lifeguard jumped into pool to save the baby.

4. Which part of the sentence is underlined?

   <u>Our family</u> went to the farm to cut down our Christmas tree.

   action part   naming part

5.   Underline the nouns that name a place.

   grocery   monkey   girl   bank   clown

6.   Use the "make capital" mark to show which words should
      begin with a capital letter.

   january   owl   monday   church   mrs.

7 – 8.   You just put a pool in your backyard. List some games
         you are going to play in the pool or some toys you will
         buy for your pool.

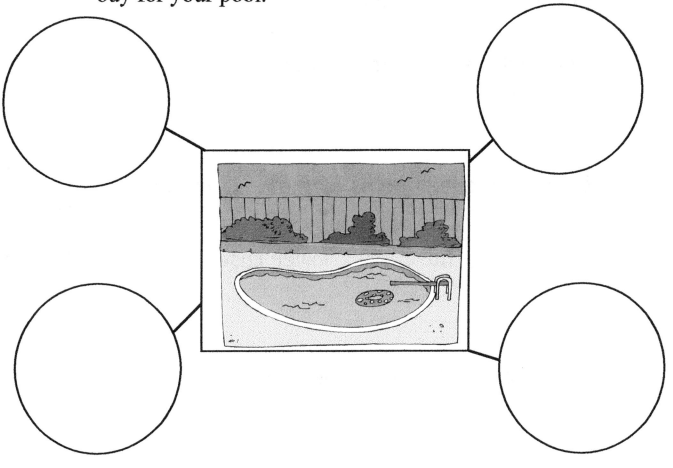

Lesson #72

1. **Some nouns show that a person owns something. When a noun names one person, you add an apostrophe (') and an "s" to the noun to show that it belongs to them.**

    Examples: Terra's hat   bird's wing   Ben's cat

    Add an apostrophe (') and an "s" to each noun to show ownership.

    boy___ room   David___ bike

    Julie___ dress

2. Fill in the correct end mark.

    Take a shower before you go to bed___

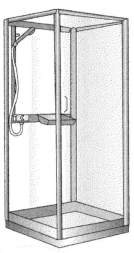

3. Every sentence begins with a _____ letter.

    capital   lower case

4. Write the mark for "add something."   _____

5. Use a pronoun to take the place of the underlined words. (Use *he*, *she*, *they*, or *it*.)

   <u>My mom and dad</u> let me have a slumber party.

   _____

6. Which word has a spelling mistake? Write the correct spelling below.

   clim   there   long

   _____

7. Write the sentence with corrections.

   mrs. Hanson is moving⋀Texas ⊙
   ≡   to

   _____

   _____

8. Which words have a long vowel sound?

   feet   cup   make   tin   time

Lesson #73

1.   Which words have the same vowel sound?

         lazy   hide   make   boat   gave

2.   Underline the action part of this sentence.

     Eva and Frankie ran to the swings.

3.   Write the two words that make up this compound word.

     drumstick ➡ _____ + _____

4.   Write this sentence correctly.

     miss Jenkins is my Math teacher.

     _____

     _____

5.   Use a pronoun to take the place of the underlined words. (Use *he, she, they,* or *it.*)

<u>Mitch and Greg</u> got in trouble on the playground.

_____

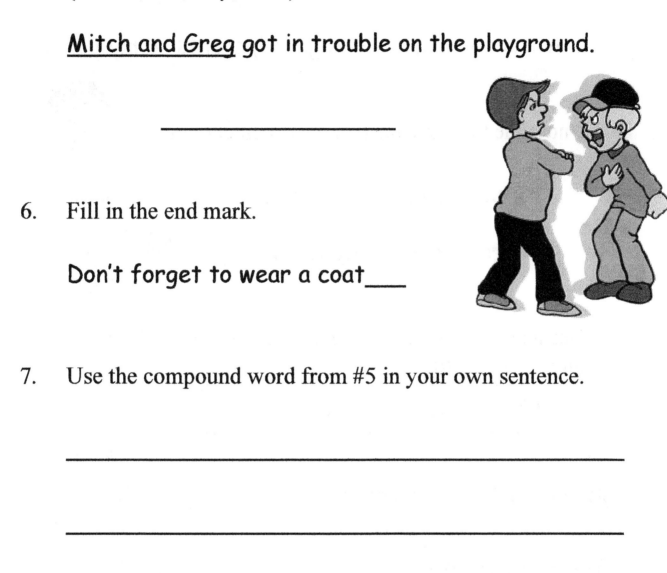

6.   Fill in the end mark.

Don't forget to wear a coat___

7.   Use the compound word from #5 in your own sentence.

_____

_____

8.   **When a noun names one person, you add an apostrophe (') and an "*s*" to the noun to show that it belongs to them.** Add an apostrophe (') and an "*s*" to each noun to show ownership.

Anne___ socks   Peter___ mouse

Lesson #74

1.   Underline the nouns that name people.

I invited my cousins and grandparents to my party.

2.   Underline the sentence that is written correctly.

I and Carmen play tennis.

Carmen and I play tennis.

3.   Use a pronoun from the box to take the place of the underlined words.

he	they	she	it

My sister loves ice cream. _____

The bus was late. _____

Joe rode his bike to the park. _____

4.   Nouns name people, places, or things.

true   false

5.　Use the mark for "add something" to fix this sentence.

I heard funny joke.

6.　Rewrite the sentence in #5 correctly.

_____

7 – 8.　List some places you would like to go to on summer vacation.

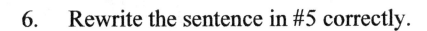

Lesson #75

1.   Make these words mean more than one.

   drum ➡ _____

   boat ➡ _____

2.   Underline the nouns that name things.

   Ian likes to read books and work puzzles.

3.   Underline the action part of the sentence.

   The children built a snowman.

4.   Use capital letters correctly.

   friday - _____

   march - _____

   halloween - _____

5 – 6. Look back at the last lesson. Choose <u>one</u> place you would like to visit over summer break. Write two or three sentences telling why you'd like to visit that place.

_____

_____

_____

_____

7. Add an apostrophe (') and an "*s*" to each noun to show the object belongs to them.

child____ kite

baby____ toy

8. Write the compound word from sentence #3 in this lesson.

_____

Lesson #76

1. **Most times we add "*s*" to make nouns name more than one. We add "*es*" to nouns that end in *s, x, z, ch*, and *sh*.**

    Example: class ➡ class<u>es</u>   beach ➡ beach<u>es</u>
    wish ➡ wish<u>es</u>   fox ➡ fox<u>es</u>

    Make each noun name more than one.

    peach _____   box _____

2. Which word has a spelling mistake? Write the correct spelling on the line.

    across   even   agian

    _____

3. Which word means the opposite of the word *float*?

    float ➡   swim   sink   dive

4.   Underline the sentence that is written correctly.

We flew out of cleveland on monday.

We flew out of Cleveland on Monday.

5.   Circle the noun that names a thing.

pencil   girl   church

6.   Underline the proper noun in this sentence.

Our class studied about Japan.

7.   Add the marks for "make capital" and "add something" to fix the sentence.

sherry is babysitter.

8.   Write the mark for "make lower case." _____

Lesson #77

1. **We add "*es*" to nouns that end in *s*, *x*, *z*, *ch*, and *sh*.**

    Make each noun name more than one.

    wish - _____   watch - _____

2. Rewrite this sentence.

    On tuesday my Dad went out of town⊙

    _____

    _____

3. Which word means the same as the word *cold*?

    cold ➡   angry   chilly   yell

4. Every sentence begins with a _____ letter.

    lower case   capital

5.   Underline the proper noun.

My friend Melissa wrote me a letter.

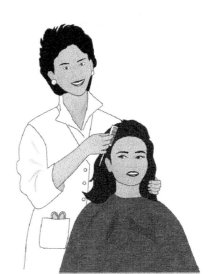

6.   Which sentence is written correctly?

Me and Jason went out for pizza.

Jason and I went out for pizza.

7.   Fill in the end mark.

Who cuts your hair___

8.   Choose a pronoun from the Word Box to take the place of
      the underlined noun in the sentence.

┌─────────────────────────────────────┐
│   He   They   She   │
└─────────────────────────────────────┘

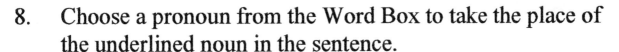

Tonya won a gold fish. _____

My aunt and uncle moved across the street. _____

Lesson #78

1.   Add an apostrophe (') and an "*s*" to each noun to show ownership.

   girl___ doll   Jenny___ notebook

2.   Draw a line under the noun in each sentence. A noun may name a person, a place, or a thing. There are 2 nouns in each sentence.

   The scouts slept in a tent.

   Our dog has his own house.

3.   Write a pronoun to take the place of "*The scouts*" in the sentence above.

   _____

4.   Underline the word that makes the sentence correct.

   He ate four (apple / apples).

5. Which word has a spelling mistake? Write the word correctly.

> would   where   pleas

_____

6. Use the mark for "add something" and "add a period" to fix this sentence.

Justin scored winning goal

7. Use *'s* to show ownership.

mom___ plate   Jared___magazine

8. Tell whether each word has a long or a short vowel sound.

team _____

fire _____

last _____

Lesson #79

1. **When a noun names more than one and already ends in "s," just add an apostrophe (') to show ownership.**

    Example: birds' nests   cousins' yard

    Add an apostrophe to the nouns that name more than one to show ownership.

    friends__ books   sisters__ bikes

2. **We add "es" to nouns that end in s, x, z, ch, and sh.**

    Make each noun name more than one.

    lunch - _____

    bus - _____

3. Which part of the sentence is underlined?

    Robert <u>learned to play the drums</u>.

    naming part   action part

4 – 5.   Write three sentences about the picture below. Tell why these children are so happy. Be sure to include end marks.

_____

_____

_____

_____

6.   Underline the group of words that make a sentence.

Played soccer.

Our next game is Saturday.

7.   Which word is a synonym for (means almost the same as) the word *fast*?

fast ➡   quick   slow   touch

8.   Write the mark that shows "add a period."   _____

Lesson #80

1.   Fill in the end mark.

Yea, our team won___

Please feed the dog___

2.   **When a noun names more than one and already ends in "s," just add an apostrophe (') to show ownership.**

Add an apostrophe to the nouns that name more than one to show ownership.

monkeys___ bananas   parents___ car

3.   Write the two words that make up the compound word *fingernail*.

_____ + _____

4.   Choose the words that make this sentence correct.

(Me and Randy / Randy and I) collect rocks.

5.   Choose the correct word to show ownership.

A (lion's / lions') paw is hurt.

My (dad's / dads') office is downtown.

6.   Circle the words that have a short vowel sound.

sister   tire   fix   tick   bite

7.   Choose a pronoun to take the place of the
      underlined words. (Use *he, she, they,* or *it.*)

The car had a flat tire.   _____

Paco fixed the tire.   _____

8.   Rewrite this sentence correctly.

stan enjoyed the play⊙

Lesson #81

1.   A noun can name a person, a _____, or a thing.

   compound   place   vowel

2.   Underline the sentence that is correct.

   Are your keys in your sisters' purse?

   Are your keys in your sister's purse?

3.   Underline the telling part of the sentence.

   The pony jumped the fence.

4.   Find the proper noun in the sentence. Rewrite the proper noun with a capital letter.

   The pony's name is felicia.

   _____

5.   Which word means the opposite of the word *up*?

up   ➡   high   go   down

6.   Circle the two nouns in this sentence.

My neighbor is a dentist.

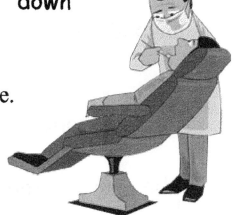

7 – 8.   **When you write sentences, read them over to make
           sure they make sense and they are in the right order.**

Number these sentences to show the correct order.

_____ Finally, I put the pan in the oven.

_____ Then, I put the batter in a pan.

_____ First, I get out a bowl.

_____ Then, I put eggs and the cake mix in the bowl.

_____ Next, I mix everything together.

Lesson #82

1.   Write the two words that make up this compound word.

anybody ➡ _____ + _____

2.   Circle the correct word.

The men painted the (porches / porchs).

Her jeans had three (patchs / patches).

3.   Fill in the correct end mark.

Did she lose her ring____

4.   Use the marks for "make capital" and "add something" to fix this sentence.

Her cousin got new skates christmas.

5.   Underline the noun in each row.

A) eat   small   girl

B) go   football   stop

C) three   like   goat

6.   Which word has a spelling mistake? Write the word
     correctly.

these   under   somthing

_____

7.   Use capital letters correctly.

august - _____

mr. - _____

new year's day - _____

8.   Write the mark for "make lower case."   _____

Lesson #83

1. **When a noun names more than one and already ends in "s," just add an apostrophe (') to show ownership.**

    Add an apostrophe to the nouns that name more than one to show ownership.

    uncles__ jobs   dogs__ bowls

2. Underline the nouns that name places.

    Diane went to the drugstore

    and the bank.

3. Write the two words that make up the word *drugstore*.

    _____ + _____

4. Choose a pronoun to take the place of the underlined words. (Use *he*, *she*, *they*, or *it*.)

    <u>The nurse</u> gave me a shot.

    _____

5.   Which word means almost the same thing as the word *over*?

over ➡   above   under   below

6.   Circle the correct word.

Kerry and (me / I) are both the oldest.

7 – 8.   Write 2 good things and 2 bad things about dinosaurs
         living in the world today.

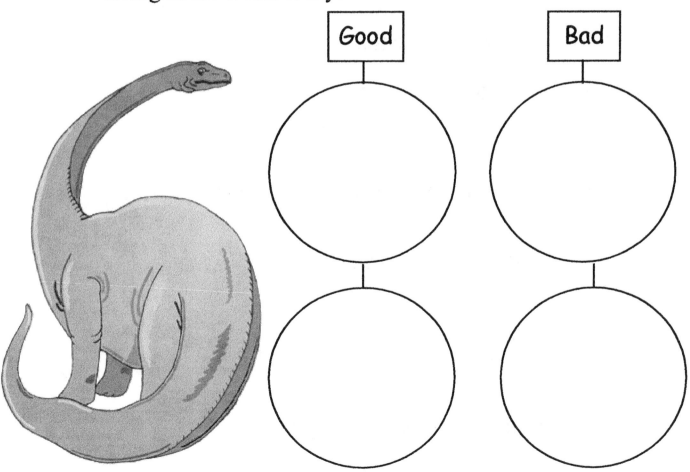

Good

Bad

Lesson #84

1. **Sometimes when you're writing you put extra words in your sentences by mistake. This is the mark that tells you to "take something out." ( )**

   Example: The cow was eating the the grass.

   Use the new mark to show which word should be taken out of the sentence below.

   We wanted a a salad for lunch.

2. Circle the correct word.

   The (farmer's / farmers')

   chicken laid many eggs.

3. A noun can name people, places, or things.

   true   false

4. Fill in the correct end mark.

   Be home on time for supper__

5. Make these nouns name more than one. Watch the ending of each word.

church - _____

whale - _____

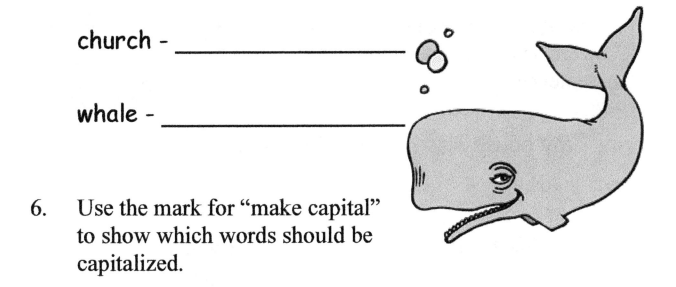

6. Use the mark for "make capital" to show which words should be capitalized.

my uncle works every saturday and sunday.

7. Underline the naming part of the sentence.

The baby pig played in the mud.

8. Underline the word group that makes a sentence.

Carl always wins at checkers.

Chased the ball.

Lesson #85

1. **This is the mark that tells you to "take something out." (⌐)**

   Use the new mark to show which word should be taken out of the sentence.

   My house sits high on the a hill.

2. Underline the nouns in this sentence. (There are 3.)

   The teacher helped the student

   do her worksheet.

3. Write this sentence correctly.

   On friday we will take∧ field trip⊙
                         a

   _____

   _____

4.   Use the Word Box to make 2 compound words.

| cracker | light | fire | moon |

_____

_____

5.   Add an *apostrophe* + *–s* (*'s*) to show ownership.

Gina__ scooter   dad__ office

6 – 8.   Look back at Lesson #83. Write three
         sentences telling the good things and bad
         things about dinosaurs living today.

_____

_____

_____

_____

Lesson #86

1. Which words have the same vowel sound?

   three   cage   fight   take   fat

2. Circle the words that are correct.

   (Me and James / James and I)

   erased the board.

3. Write the mark that matches the definition.

   take something out - _____

   add something - _____

   make lower case - _____

4. A pronoun takes the place of a noun.

   true   false

5.   Choose the correct word to show ownership.

The (workers' / worker's) hammer was left

on the ground.

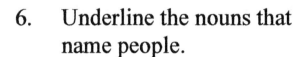

6.   Underline the nouns that
      name people.

The doctor told the nurse to give me a shot.

7.   Add "*s*" or "*es*" to make these words mean more than one.

five peach____   four pencil____   two paper____

8.   Write this sentence correctly.

We went to the /musement park⊙

_____

_____

Lesson #87

1.   Circle the word that rhymes with *street.*

bite   treat   great

2.   **A verb is a word that names an action that someone does or did.   You will find the verb in the action part of the sentence.**

Example: The fish <u>jumped</u> out of the water.
"Jumped out of the water" is the action part of the sentence. The word "jumped" is the verb.

Underline the verb in the sentence.

Hannah walked to her grandma's house.

3.   Fill in the end mark.

Where did you go on vacation____

4.   Which word means almost the same as the word *shut*?

shut ➡ open   close   fly

5.   Use the marks for "take something out" and "make capital" to fix this sentence.

On tuesday my dad and I are going go fishing.

6.   Underline the naming part of this sentence.

Mr. Jacobs put a fence in his yard.

7.   Underline the proper nouns.

Monica   boat   Cleveland   baseball

8.   Underline any groups of words that make a sentence.

Dropped the ball.

Niki told a joke.

My dad.

We had ice cream and cake.

Lesson #88

1.   **A verb is a word that names an action that someone does or did. You will find the verb in the action part of the sentence.**

Look at the action part of the sentence. What word tells what the snake did?

The snake crawled in the grass.

2.   Which word has a spelling mistake?

grow   anamil   began

3.   Write the correct spelling on the line.

_____

4.   Use a pronoun (*he*, *she*, *it*, or *they*) to take the place of the underlined words.

<u>The snail</u> moved slowly.   _____

<u>Frankie</u> loves football.   _____

<u>My grandparents</u> live out of town. _____

5.   Circle the correct word.

Janet and (I / me) are on the soccer

team.

6 – 7.   **After you make your writing better, fix your mistakes by using the special marks.** This part of writing is called **proofreading**.

Write this sentence correctly.

My dad planted Ṫulips in ∧backyard⊙
                               the

_____

_____

8.   Write the two words that make up the compound word in #7.

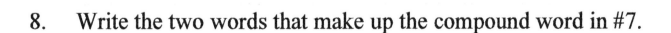

_____ + _____

Lesson #89

1. Underline the action word in the sentence. (What word tells what the panda bears do?)

    Panda bears eat plants and

    small animals.

2. Write the naming part of the sentence in #1.

    _____

3 – 4. List the directions for making a peanut butter and jelly sandwich. (They don't have to be in the correct order.)

    1)_____

    2)_____

    3)_____

    4)_____

    5)_____

5.   Which word rhymes with *show?*

              sing   does   grow

6.   Which word means the opposite of the word *right?*

       right ➡ wrong   kind   funny

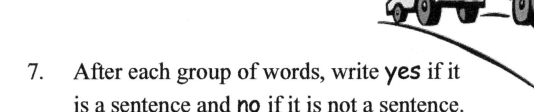

7.   After each group of words, write **yes** if it
      is a sentence and **no** if it is not a sentence.

      He hit another car. _____

      He called a tow truck. _____

      The police. _____

8.   Circle the correct word to show ownership.

      (Sasha's / Sashas') plant needs water.

Lesson #90

1. Use the "take something out" mark to show which word should be taken out of the sentence.

    He had to pack for his his trip.

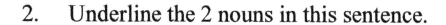

2. Underline the 2 nouns in this sentence.

    He chased his dog down the street.

3. Circle the verb in the sentence. What word tells what Carol did?

    Carol mowed the lawn.

4. Fill in the correct end mark.

    Give the dog a bath___

    Where is the shampoo___

    It is in the basement___

5.   Underline the sentence that has no mistake.

Love to camp!

We went camping on saturday.

I put up the Tent.

Do you like to camp?

6.   A pronoun takes the place of a noun.

         true   false

7 – 8. Look back at yesterday's lesson (question #3 – 4). Put the
         steps to making the peanut butter and jelly sandwich in the
         correct order.

1)_____

2)_____

3)_____

4)_____

5)_____

Lesson #91

1.   Use words from the Word Box to make 2 compound words.

tooth   fly   brush   butter

_____

_____

2.   Add a naming part to this sentence.

_____ live in the water.

3.   Underline the verb in the sentence.
      What word tells what the class did?

      The class hiked up the hill.

4.   A noun names a person, place, or thing.

        true   false

5. Add "*s*" or "*es*" to each word to make it name more than one.

    three bus_____

    six hat_____

    nine dish_____

6. Use the mark for "make capital" and "take something out" to fix this sentence.

mr. Grubber coaches baseball on every friday.

7. Write a proper noun for each one.

girl - _____

school - _____

state - _____

8. Months, days of the week, and holidays begin with a capital letter.

        true   false

Lesson #92

1. Use a pronoun (*he*, *she*, *it*, or *they*) to take the place of the underlined words.

Felipe fixes cars. _____

The truck tipped over. _____

2. Fill in the end mark.

Ouch, that hurt___

Can you hear me___

3. Circle the correct word.

(I and Kim / Kim and I) listened to music.

4. Which word means the same as the word *high*?

high ➡ tall   low   bad

5.   Circle the nouns.

      flower   hopped   sing   wheel   pen

6.   **A prefix comes at the beginning of a word. It changes the meaning of the word. The prefix *un–* means "not."**

      Example: <u>un</u>happy means "not happy"
                     <u>un</u>able means "not able"

      Use one of the examples above to complete the sentence.

      Alice was _____ to tie her shoes.

7 – 8.   Write the mark that matches the definition.

      take something out - _____

      add something - _____

      make lower case - _____

      make capital - _____

      add a period - _____

Lesson #93

1. **A prefix comes at the beginning of a word. It changes the meaning of the word. The prefix *un–* means "not."**

   Make a new word using the prefix *un–* and the word *tie*.

   un- + tie ➡ _____

2. Underline the naming part of the sentence.

   The owl looks for food at night.

3. Write a pronoun to take the place of *The owl* in #2.

   _____

4. Underline the verb in each sentence.

   The frog jumped into the pond.

   I chopped wood for the fire.

5.   Use the mark for "make capital" to show which words in the
      sentence should begin with a capital letter.

      jamal jogs every wednesday and saturday.

6.   Which words have a short vowel sound?

      pie   best   goat   get

7.   Circle the correct word.

      The (houses' / house's) roofs leaked.

8.   Write this sentence correctly.

          the baby smiled ∧ me.
                          at

_____

Lesson #94

1.   Underline the noun in each row.

    A) shell   work   skip

    B) throw   sad   drum

    C) red   bakery   see

2.   **Verbs can tell if an action is happening now. Add an "*s*" to this kind of verb when the noun names one.**

Example: The cat walks.   Anna jumps.   Andy runs.

Choose the correct verb in each sentence.

    The dog (find / finds) a bone.

    The frog (hop / hops) away.

3.   Make a new word using the prefix *un–* and the word *do.*

    un- + do ➡ _____

4.   Write the mark for "take something out." _____

5. Underline the action part of this sentence. Then, circle the verb in the action part.

    Delvon drew a picture of a lake.

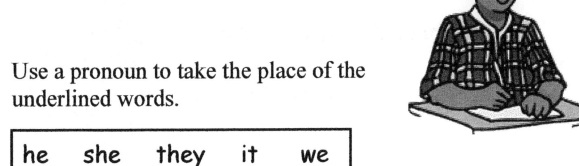

6. Use a pronoun to take the place of the underlined words.

    | he   she   they   it   we |

    Aunt Judy came for dinner. _____

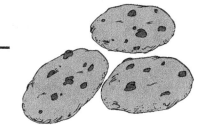

    Barry loves cookies. _____

    My sister and I went sled riding. _____

7. Write the 2 words that make up the compound word below.

    snowflake ➡ _____ + _____

8. Circle the correct word.

    This is my (dad's / dads') hat.

Lesson #95

1. **Verbs can tell if an action is happening now. Add an "*s*" to this kind of verb when the noun names one.**

   Choose the correct verb in each sentence.

   Mom (bake / bakes) a cake.

   Juanita (love / loves) pickles.

2. Which word is an antonym (means "the opposite") of the word *break*?

   break ➡ spend   fix   work

3. Use the marks for "add a period" and "make lower case" to fix this sentence.

   We picked a Sunflower from

   our garden

4. Add "*s*" or "*es*" to make these nouns name more than one.

   rabbit____   crutch____   dish ____

5.   Underline the noun in the sentence.

    The gate is closed.

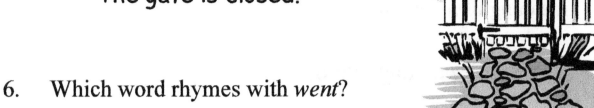

6.   Which word rhymes with *went*?

    were   cute   sent

7 – 8.   Think of a story that goes with the picture. Fill in the
chart with the five W's.

Who?	What?	Where?

When?	Why?

Lesson #96

1. Add the prefix *un–* to the word *cooked*. The new word is *uncooked*. The prefix *un-* means "not." What is the meaning of *uncooked*?

   The meat was <u>uncooked</u>. _____

2. Use a pronoun to replace the underlined words.

   <u>The women</u> in the picture are sisters. _____

3. Fill in the correct end mark.

   How old are they___

   They don't look alike____

4. **A suffix is added to the end of a word. It changes the meaning of the word. The suffix *–ful* means "full of."**

   Example: <u>thankful</u> means "full of thanks"

   What does the word *joyful* mean?

   _____

5. **Add an "*s*" to this kind of verb when the noun names one.**

Choose the correct verb in each sentence.

The little girl (skip / skips) to school.

My brother (play / plays) in the clubhouse.

6. Underline the verb in the sentence.

The baby cried all night.

7. Write the naming part of the sentence in #6.

_____

8. Which word has a spelling mistake? Spell the word correctly on the line.

change   buzy   baby

_____

Lesson #97

1. **Some verbs tell that an action is happening now. Other verbs tell actions that happened in the past or before now. Add _–ed_ to most verbs to show that an action has happened in the past.**

    Example: Today Thomas <u>walks</u> in the woods. (Now)
    Yesterday Thomas <u>walked</u> in the woods. (Past)

    Add _–ed_ to each verb to show that it happened in the past.

    play_____   look_____   pick_____

2. Underline the nouns that name places.

    We stopped at the bakery and the post office.

3. Use capitals correctly.

    mr. _____

    july _____

4. Circle the correct answer.

    (Connie and me / Connie and I) ate soup for lunch.

5. Underline the proper noun.

    We live in Florida.

6. Write this sentence correctly.

    mrs. johnson has a house on the Ocean.

    _____

    _____

7. Which word means almost the same as the word *yummy*?

    yummy ➡ small   pretty   delicious

8. A **suffix** is added to the **end of a word.** It changes the
    meaning of the word. The suffix *–ful* means "full of."
    What does the word *careful* mean?

    _____

Lesson #98

1. **Add _-ed_ to most verbs to show that an action has happened in the past.**

    Circle the verb that tells about the past.

    I (colors / colored) a picture.

    We (bounces / bounced) the ball.

2. Underline the action part of the sentence.

    She ran after the bus.

3. Put these two words together to make a compound word.

    door + knob ➡ _____ _____

4. Add an _apostrophe + –s_ ('s) to show ownership.

    bird____ nest   Muffy____ cage

5 – 6. Look back at Lesson #95. Write 3
        sentences about the picture. Use
        the five W's boxes to help you.

_____

_____

_____

_____

_____

7.   Fill in the end mark.

     An ostrich cannot fly____

     Is it a bird____

8.   Underline the group of words that makes a sentence.

         We cleaned the attic.

         Baked an apple pie.

Lesson #99

1.　Add the suffix *–ful* to each word.　Write the new word.

　　peace + -ful ➡ _____

　　play + -ful ➡ _____

2.　Circle the verb to show that
　　it happened in the past.

　　James (shoveled / shovels) the snow.

3.　Use a pronoun to take the place of the
　　underlined words. (*we*, *they*, *he*, *she*, *it*)

　　<u>My cousin and I</u> don't have any juice.　_____

　　<u>Marissa</u> jumped rope.　_____

4.　A noun names people, places, or things.

　　　　true　　　　　　false

5.   The prefix *un–* means "not." What does *uncovered* mean?

    _____

6.   Use the mark for "make capital" to show which words
     should begin with a capital letter. (There are 3.)

     gayle came over for thanksgiving dinner on thursday.

7.   Circle the correct verb.

     The bunny (hop / hops)

     around the yard.

8.   Tell whether each word has a **long** vowel sound or a **short**
     vowel sound.

     have - _____   hive - _____

     teach - _____   jump - _____

Lesson #100

1. Use the mark for "take something out" to fix this sentence.

    At the zoo the seals put on on a show.

2. Underline the sentence that
    is a command.

    What are you doing after lunch? We are going to

    the movies. Ask your mom if you can come with us.

3. Add the suffix *–ful* to make a word that means "full of care."

    care + -ful ➡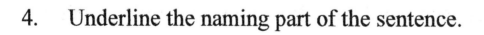

4. Underline the naming part of the sentence.

    Mrs. Conner drives our bus.

5. Look at the sentence in #4. Write the verb on the line. What
    word tells what Mrs. Conner does?

    _____

6 – 7. Use the Word Web to tell some things about your favorite television show.

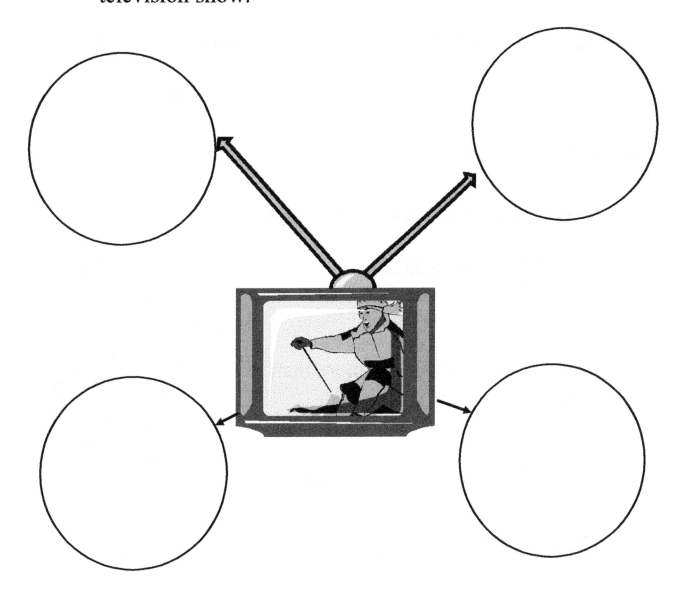

8. A prefix comes at the _____ of a word.

   beginning   end

Lesson #101

1. Underline the nouns.

    bird   catch   truck   bank   yell

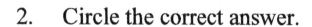

2. Circle the correct answer.

    (Frankie and I / Me and Frankie)

    are in the same class.

3. Make these nouns name more than
    one by adding "*s*" or "*es*."

    team ➡ _____

    sandwich ➡ _____

4. Circle the words that rhyme with *goat*.

    have   float   boat   glove   coat

5.   Underline the verb in the action part of the sentence.

The beavers built a nest in

the water.

6.   Use a pronoun to take the place of the underlined words. (Use *he, she, we, they,* or *it.*)

Mr. Ling is my violin teacher. _____

7 – 8.   Look back at the Word Web in Lesson #100. Write three sentences about your favorite television program.

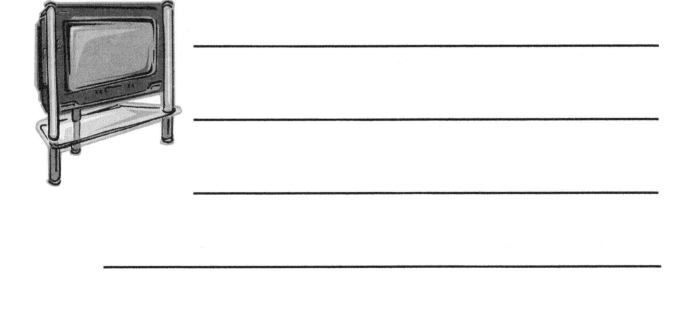

Lesson #102

1. **Sometimes verbs need a helping word like *has* or *have* to show past time. *Has* and *have* are called *helping verbs*.**

   Example: The game <u>has started</u>.
   We <u>have played</u> the game many times.

   Choose *has* or *have* to finish each sentence.

   We (has / have) found her book.

   Dave (has / have) read that book already.

2. Underline the action part of the sentence.

   Grandpa fed the little baby.

3. Write the sentence correctly.

   <u>there</u> are a lot of stars in⋀ sky ⊙
   =
                                          the

   _____

4. Fill in the end mark.

    An ape is not a pet____

    Does it live in the zoo____

5. Which word is the opposite of the word *wild*?

    wild ➡   tame   afraid   sleepy

6. Circle the correct verb.

    The squirrel (run / runs) along the lake.

7. A telling sentence and a command
    end with a period.

        true   false

8. Add the prefix *un–* to the word *afraid* to make a word that
    means "not afraid."

        un- + afraid ➡ _____

Lesson #103

1. Underline the verb in the action part of this sentence.

    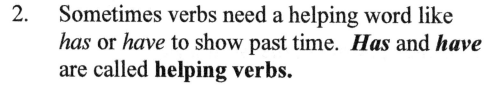 The boys dried the dishes.

2. Sometimes verbs need a helping word like
    has or *have* to show past time. **Has** and **have**
    are called **helping verbs.**

    Choose *has* or *have* in each sentence.

    The eagle (has / have) flapped its wings.

    The children (has / have) finished their dinner.

3. Write a pronoun to take the place of the
    underlined noun.

    <u>Robots</u> can do many things. _____

4. **The prefix *re–* means "again."** Add the prefix *re–* to the
    word *copy* to make a word that means "copy again."

    re- + copy ➡ _____

5. Which word has a spelling mistake? Write the word correctly on the line.

    cach   night   guess

    _____

6. Use the mark for "make capital" to show which words should begin with a capital letter.

    every christmas scott goes to florida.

7. Circle the correct verb to show past time.

    Leo (snap / snapped) the picture.

8. Read each group of words. Underline the sentence.

    Sent a letter.

    My sisters.

    Brent saw a woodpecker.

Lesson #104

1. The prefix *re–* means **"again."** Add the prefix *re–* to the word below to make a word that means "do again."

   re- + do ➡ _____

2. *Has* and *have* are called **helping verbs.** Circle the correct verb to show past time.

   Lee (has / have) finished the report.

   The students (has / have) worked on the banner.

3. Which part of the sentence is underlined?

   <u>Mr. Piper</u> is a gardener.

   naming part   action part

4. Write a question beginning with the word below. Watch your end mark.

   What_____

5.   Which word means almost the same as the word *feel*?

       feel ➡   smart   choose   touch

6.   The nouns below name more than one.
       Add an *apostrophe* after the *–s* to show
       ownership.

       ladies___ dishes   nurses___ caps

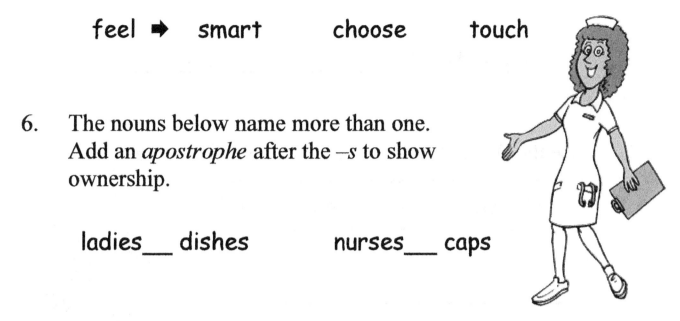

7 –8.   You are planning a Halloween party. Use the Web below
        to list some games you'll play and the food you'll eat.

Lesson #105

1. Add the suffix *–ful* to make a word that means "full of play."

    play + -ful ➡ _____

2. Use the Word Box to make two compound words.

black   house   bird   board

    _____

    _____

3. Underline the nouns that name things.

    I bought a game, some candy, and a book.

4. Circle the correct verb that shows something happening now.

    Dad (steer / steers) the boat.

5. **The last part of writing is copying your sentences neatly and sharing your words with someone else.** This is called **publishing** your work.

    The last part of writing is called _____ your work.

    fixing   publishing

6. Use the mark for "make lower case" and "add a period" to fix this sentence.

    Dale carried the Flag

7. Verbs are action words. Underline each action word.

    jump   horse   chair   hop   sing

8. **The suffix –er means "someone who does something."**

    Example: paint<u>er</u> ➡ someone who paints

    Add the suffix –er to the word *teach* to make a word that means "someone who teaches."

    teach + -er ➡ _____

Lesson #106

1. **Some verbs have a special spelling to show past time. They have different spelling when you use them with *have* and *has*.**

    Example: <u>ran</u> and <u>run</u>

    Jason <u>ran</u> in the race.
    He <u>has run</u> in that race before.

    Circle the correct verb.

    The dog (run / ran) away.

    They have (ran / run) after their dog before.

2. Use a pronoun to take the place of the underlined words.
    (Use *he, she, it, we,* or *they*.)

    <u>Grandpa and Mark</u> went fishing. _____

    <u>My cousin and I</u> stayed home to chop wood. _____

3. Every sentence begins with a capital letter.

    true   false

4. Write the mark for "make capital." _____

5. The suffix *–er* means **"someone who does something."**
    Add the suffix *–er* to the word *paint* to make a word that
    means "someone who paints."

    paint + -er ➡ _____

6. Write this sentence correctly.

    john glenn walked on the Moon.

    _____

    _____

7. Underline the verb in the action part of the sentence.

    Sal buttoned his raincoat.

8. Write the two words that make up the compound word in #7.

    _____ + _____

Lesson #107

1. **Some verbs have a special spelling to show past time. They have another spelling when you use them with *have* and *has*. Example:** <u>came</u> and <u>has come</u> / <u>have come</u>

    > Uncle Ted <u>came</u> to my game.
    > Many other people <u>have come</u>, too.

    Circle the correct verb.

    Louis (came / come) to visit me last night.

    The puppies have (come / came) back home.

2. Add an *apostrophe* + *–s* to make the single nouns show ownership.

    plant__ seeds   bird__ beak

3. Make these words mean more than one by adding "*s*" or "*es*."

    barn - _____

    bench - _____

4. Use the marks for "add something" and "take something out" to fix this sentence.

    Rasheed is good good swimmer.

5. Add the prefix *re–* to the word *clean* to make a word that means "clean again."

    re- + clean ➡ _____

6. Underline the correct sentence.

    Me and Christine planted flowers.

    Christine and I planted flowers.

7. Which words have a long vowel sound?

    back   tie   snow   jump   seed

8. Underline the proper nouns.

    My brother, John, has a friend named Harry.

Lesson #108

1. Add the suffix *–er* to the word *fight* to make a word that means "someone who fights."

    fight + -er ➡ _____

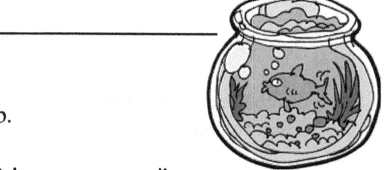

2. Circle the correct verb.

    She (hug / hugged) her mom goodbye.

    Diego (drop / dropped) the fish bowl.

3. Underline the naming part of the sentence.

    Kiely chewed a hole in the hose.

4. Fill in the correct end mark.

    Yea, we are winning____

    Why are you crying____

5.   Add the prefix *un–* to the word *friendly* to make a word that means "not friendly."

un- + friendly ➡ _____

6.   Some verbs have a special spelling to show past time. They have another spelling when you use them with *have* and *has*.
     Example: <u>saw</u> and <u>has seen</u> / <u>have seen</u>

          Ian <u>saw</u> some frogs by the pond.
          He <u>has seen</u> them in the yard, too.

Circle the correct verb.

We (see / saw) a funny clown yesterday.

We have (see / seen) him at other shows.

7.   Write a sentence of your own using the verb *saw*.

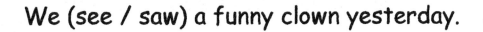

8.   Which word has a spelling mistake?

          along   ben   behind

Lesson #109

1. **The verbs *am, is, are, was*, and *were* are verbs that do not show action. They tell what someone *is* or *was*.**

   Example: She <u>is</u> sleepy.   He <u>was</u> ill.   We <u>are</u> here.

   Choose the correct verb.

   My favorite subject (is / are) reading.

   I (is / am) getting a good grade.

   My teacher (was / were) happy.

2. Which word means the opposite of the word *down*?

   down ➡   under   up   quiet

3. Use a pronoun in place of the underlined words.

   <u>Ms. Mitchell</u> is my second grade teacher. _____

   <u>My dad and I</u> played golf. _____

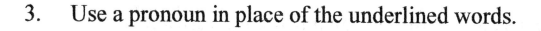

4. Write the mark for "take something out." _____

5. Some verbs have a special spelling to show past time. They have another spelling when you use them with *have* and *has*.

   Example: <u>went</u> and <u>has gone</u> / <u>have gone</u>

   Randy <u>went</u> to the park.

   He <u>has gone</u> there many times.

   Choose the correct verb.

   Darrin (went / gone) with him.

   Mark had (went / gone) to the store.

6. Underline the action part of this sentence.

   William reads the newspaper after dinner.

7. Underline the sentence that asks a question.

   My dad and I went hunting. We were

   looking for deer. Did you catch anything?

   Wow, we caught two deer!

8. Circle the sentence above that is an exclamation.

Lesson #110

1. The verbs *am, is, are, was,* and *were* are verbs that **do not show action. They tell what someone *is* or *was*.**

   Choose the correct verb.

   I (is / am) the boss.

   Nina (was / were) the boss before me.

2. Write the two words that make up the compound word.

   notebook ➡ _____ + _____

3. Add an *apostrophe* after the *–s* to show ownership when the noun names more than one.

   dogs__ bones   clowns__ balloons

4. Make these nouns name more than one by adding "*s*" or "*es*."

   jacket____   sled____   bush____

5. **The prefix _pre–_ means "before."**
    Example: <u>Pregame</u> means "before the game."

    Add the prefix _pre–_ to the word _school_ to
    make a word that means "before school."

    pre- + school ➡ _____

6. Use the word _preschool_ in a sentence.

    _____

7. Underline the correct verb.

    Josh (hammer / hammered) the board.

8. Circle the noun in each row.

    A) bug   sweep   laugh

    B) sad   grandma   pretty

    C) give   saw   ruler

Lesson #111

1. A prefix comes at the beginning of a word.

   true   false

2. Use the mark for "make capital" and "add something" to fix this sentence.

   We go lewis School.

3. The prefix *pre–* means **"before."** Add the prefix *pre–* to the word *pay* to make a word that means "before paying."

   pre- + pay ➡ _____

4. Underline the sentence.

   Water bugs.

   We had company for dinner.

   Played in the basement all day.

5.   Underline the action part of the sentence.

Mario combed his hair.

6.   Write the proper noun from the sentence in #5.

_____

7.   Choose the correct verb.

The outside light (was / were) left on.

My cousins (is / are) coming for dinner.

8.   Tell about your favorite kind of weather. Use the special
     marks to fix any mistakes.

_____

_____

_____

_____

Lesson #112

1. A **contraction** is a **shorter way of writing two words.**
    Some letters are left out in the new word and an
    apostrophe **takes the place** of those letters.

    Example: did not ➡ didn't   is not ➡ isn't
                   does not ➡ doesn't   do not ➡ don't

    Write the contraction for each.

    did not ➡ _____

    do not ➡ _____

    is not ➡ _____

2. Underline the correct verb.

    Children (play / plays) football.

    I (catch / catches) the ball.

3. Write the two words that make up the compound word in #2.

    _____ + _____

4 – 5. Read these sentences. Find and fix three mistakes using
          the special marks you have learned.

Today is my Birthday. I ran downstairs to see my

cake? My mom hid the in the cupboard. I can't wait

to see what kind of cake she made me.

6. Underline the sentence above that
     is written correctly.

7. Fill in the end mark.

Please turn out the light___

Has anyone seen my slippers___

Here comes the storm___

8. Write each word correctly.

mrs. – _____

september – _____

Lesson #113

1. **A contraction is a shorter way of writing two words.**
    Some letters are left out in the new word and an apostrophe
    takes the place of those letters.

    Write a contraction for the underlined words. (Use your Help
    Pages if you need to.)

    I <u>do not</u> know the answer. _____

    The babies <u>cannot</u> talk. _____

2. Underline the proper nouns.

    Rick lives in Texas.

3. Which word rhymes with *bunny*?

    city   candy   sunny

4. Add an *apostrophe + –s* to make a single noun show
    ownership.

    The book belongs to Sarah. It is Sarah___ book.

5. **When a word ends in a *consonant* + *y*, change the *y* to *i* and add –*es* to name more than one.**

    Example: baby ➡ babies   bunny ➡ bunnies

    Change *y* to *i* and add –*es* to show more than one.

    lady ➡ _____

    city ➡ _____

6. Use a pronoun to take the place of the underlined words.

    <u>The team</u> came in second place.   _____

7. Choose the correct verb.

    I (is / am) nine years old.

    We (was / were) out late last night.

8. Which word means the opposite of the word *hard*?

    hard ➡ heavy   smooth   soft

Lesson #114

1. **When a word ends in a consonant + *y*, change the *y* to *i* and add –*es* to name more than one.**

    Change the *y* to *i* and add –*es* to each word.

    pony ➡ _____

    penny ➡ _____

2. Underline the verb.

    The children sang a song

    in the concert.

3. Write a contraction for the underlined words. (Use your Help Pages if you need to.)

    She <u>does not</u> know the answer.   _____

    I <u>cannot</u> catch a ball.   _____

4. Which word means the same as the word *friends*?

    friends ➡   cheerful   angry   buddies

5.　Circle the correct verb.

Will (throw / throws) the ball.

Sumi (catch / catches) the ball.

6.　Use the mark for "take something out" and "add a period" to fix the sentence.

There were many the stairs to climb

7.　Rewrite the sentence in #6 correctly.

_____

_____

8.　Choose the correct verb.

I (am / is) going to the basketball game.

We (was / were) so excited!

Lesson #115

1. **The suffix _–less_ means "without."**
    Example: The dog was <u>hairless</u>. He didn't have any hair.

    Add the suffix _–less_ to the word _color_ to make a word that means "without color."

    color + -less ➡ _____

2. Change the _y_ to _i_ and add _–es_ to these words.

    puppy ➡ _____

    story ➡ _____

3. Underline the naming part of the sentence.

    The parade started downtown.

4. Write the two words that make up the compound word in #3.

    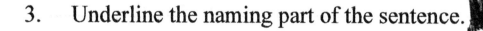

    _____ + _____

5.   Some verbs have a special spelling to show past time. They
     have another spelling when you use them with *have* and *has*.
     Example: did and has done / had done

                    He <u>did</u> a magic trick.
                    He <u>has done</u> those tricks before.

     Circle the correct verb.

     Our class (did / done) a play in reading.

     You have (did / done) a good job.

6.   Which words have the same vowel sound?

     baby   cry   hate   toad   snake

7.   Underline the nouns. (There are 2.)

     The baby bear was in a cage.

8.   Use a pronoun to take the place
     of the words *The baby bear* in
     the sentence above.

     _____

Lesson #116

1. Add an *apostrophe* + *–s* to make a single noun show ownership.

    The ball belongs to Pat. It is Pat___ ball.

2. Underline the sentence that is a telling sentence.

    Have you read your report? Please share it with the class. Wow, that is interesting! Your report was very good.

3. Underline the pronoun in each sentence.

    We did cartwheels.

    She takes dance lessons.

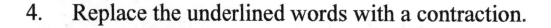

4. Replace the underlined words with a contraction.

    Ada <u>does not</u> feel well.   _____

    I <u>do not</u> know what to do.   _____

5.   Some verbs have a special spelling to show past time. They
      have another spelling when you use them with *have* and *has*.
      Example: <u>gave</u> and <u>has given</u> / <u>had given</u>
      Choose the correct verb.

      Rosa (give / gave) her report.

      Sam had (gave / given) his report already.

6.   Add the suffix *–ful* to the word *joy* to make a word that
      means "full of joy."

      joy + -ful ➡ _____

7.   Underline the action part of the sentence.
      Then, circle the verb.

      Brandon threw the basketball to John.

8.   **Whenever you write a paragraph, you should move over
      or indent the first word. This is the mark to show "move
      over" or "indent." (¶)**

      Write the mark for "move over."   _____

Lesson #117

1. Add the suffix *–er* to the word below to make a word that means "someone who sings."

   sing + -er ➡ _____

2. Fill in the end mark.

   Nora found a pine cone___

   What did she do with it___

3. Change the *y* to *i* and add *–es* to name more than one.

   family _____

4. Underline the correct sentence.

   Barry and me saw a rainbow.

   Barry and I saw a rainbow.

5.   Write the two words that make up the compound word in #4.

_____ + _____

6.   Use the mark for "move over" or "indent" to fix this
       paragraph.

       My family and I went on a long vacation. We were
       gone for three weeks. We had a great time!

7.   Write the pronoun that would take the place of *My family
       and I* in the sentence above.

_____

8.   Find three mistakes in the sentences below. Use the "special
       marks" to show how to fix them.

       I found a kitten on the road   I asked my mom

       if i could keep it. She said it would fine.

Lesson #118

1 – 2.   **Adjectives** are words that **describe** or **tell how something looks.** **Adjectives** can tell the **color**, the **size**, the **shape**, or **how many.** Use the chart to help you describe each fruit.

object	color	size	shape	how many
banana				
apple				

3.   Use the marks for "make capital" to show which words should begin with a capital letter.

   we didn't have school on labor day.

4.   Which word has a spelling mistake? Write the word correctly.

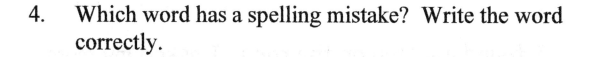

   children   mother   people

_____

5.   Underline the naming part of this sentence.

My dad gave us juice for breakfast.

6.   Which word means the opposite
       of the word *light?*

light ➡ happy   dark   color

7.   **If a word ends in –*e* and you want to add a suffix that
       begins with a vowel, drop the –*e* before adding the suffix.**

       Example: (ride + -ing)
                     We took horseback <u>riding</u> lessons.

       In each word, drop the –*e* before adding –*ing.*

       write + -ing _____

       dive + -ing _____

8.   Underline the proper nouns
       in this sentence.

Hank lives in Michigan.

Lesson #119

1 – 2. **Adjectives can also tell how something tastes or smells.
Example:** The pickle tastes sour.

Choose an adjective from the Word Box to describe each
noun below.

sweet	salty	juicy	hot

candy _____   potato chips _____

peach _____   pepper _____

3.   Add an apostrophe after the –*s* to each word that names
more than one to show ownership.

the students__ paintings   the boats__ sails

4.   Add "*s*" or "–*es*" to each word to
make it name more than one.

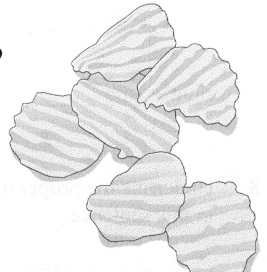

plum - _____

peach - _____

5.   Underline the verb.

Mom cooked the bacon and eggs on the stove.

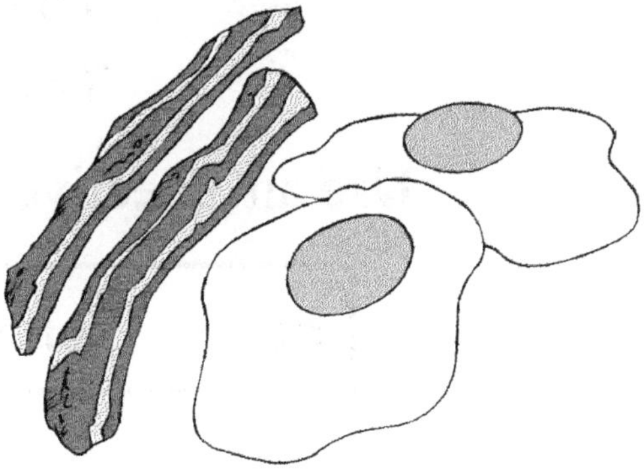

6.   Which word rhymes with *mouse*?

grow   house   mountain

7 – 8.   Draw a picture of yourself in the box. Write 3 sentences
        that tell about you.

A) _____

B) _____

C) _____

Lesson #120

1. **Adjectives** can tell how something **looks, feels,** or **sounds.**
   Example: The stove feels <u>hot</u>.
                  The milk smells <u>sour</u>.
                  The girl has a <u>loud</u> voice.

   Use an adjective from the Word Box in the sentence below.

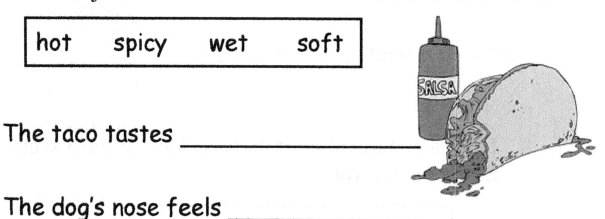

   | hot | spicy | wet | soft |

   The taco tastes _____

   The dog's nose feels _____

2. Underline the nouns in this sentence. (There are 3.)

   We found pictures of a dragonfly in our book.

3. Write the two words that make up the compound word in #2.

   _____ + _____

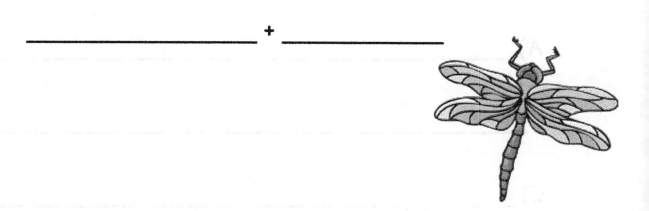

4.   Nouns name people, places, or things.

          true   false

5.   Choose the correct verb.

I (is / am) staying up late today.

We (was / were) going to play games.

6.   Write a contraction for the underlined words.
     Use your Help Pages.

Evan <u>cannot</u> find his toothbrush. _____

My sister <u>is not</u> riding the bus. _____

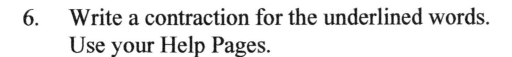

7.   Every sentence begins with a _____ letter.

        capital   lower case

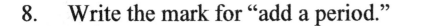

8.   Write the mark for "add a period."   _____

Lesson #121

1. Use a pronoun to replace the underlined words.

   <u>The shovel</u> is by the shed. _____

2. Write this sentence correctly.

   I have a /Hockey game on saturday⊙

   _____

   _____

3. Circle the word that means almost the same as (synonym) the word *fast*.

   fast ➡ slow   quick   cry

4. Underline the action part of the sentence.

   Todd raked leaves yesterday.

5.   Write the verb in #4 that shows past time.

      _____

6.   Use any adjective to describe the car in this sentence.
      (Adjectives can tell how it looks or sounds.)

      A _____ car raced down my street.

7.   Add the prefix *re–* to the word
      say to make a word that means
      "to say again."

      re- + say ➡ _____

8.   Write the sentence that is a command on the lines below.

      We are having a garage sale today. We have lots of

      things to sell. Go home and get your money.

      _____

      _____

Lesson #122

1. Choose the correct verb.

    Tyler (has picked / have picked) some berries.

2. Use an adjective from the Word Box to
    describe each noun.

    | cold | slippery | wet | hard |

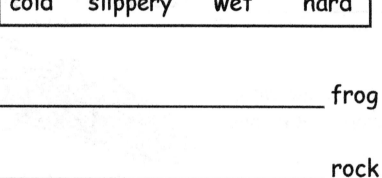

    _____ frog

    _____ rock

3. Which words have a long vowel sound?

    great   feet   itch   better

4. Fill in the end mark.

    What a great game____

    Whose sweater is this____

5. Write **yes** if the word group makes a sentence and **no** if it
    does not make a sentence.

    A) I bought a toy at the store. _____

    B) Played with it all day. _____

    C) I like. _____

    D) I will let you play with it, too. _____

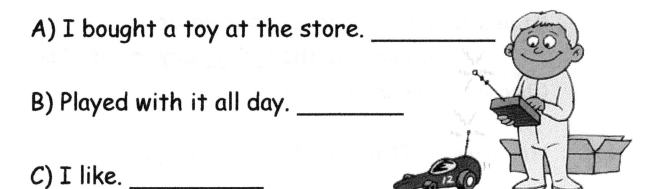

6. Use the mark for "make capital" and "add
    something" to fix the sentence.

    nina lives my street.

7. Use your corrections to write the sentence in #6 correctly.

    _____

8. Underline the proper nouns.

    My sister Nancy lives in California.

Lesson #123

1. **Add –*er* to adjectives to compare two people or things.
    Add –*est* to compare more than two people.**

    Example: Jason is <u>taller</u> than Peter.
    Michael is the <u>tallest</u> boy in the class.

    Choose the correct adjective.

    Her horse is (faster / fastest) than mine.

    My mom's horse is the (fastest / faster) of all.

2. Underline the words that should
    begin with a capital letter.

    shark   july   friday   animal   halloween

3. **If a word ends in –*e* and you want to add a suffix that
    begins with a vowel, drop the –*e* before adding the suffix.**

    In each word, drop the –*e* before adding –*ing*.

    dance +-ing ➡ _____

    smile + -ing ➡ _____

4. Add an *apostrophe* + *–s* to each noun to show ownership.

The castle belongs to the king.

It is the king___ castle.

5. Use a pronoun to take the place of the underlined words.

Darrin had a bowl of soup.   _____

A bat came down the chimney.   _____

6. Change the *y* to *i* before adding *–es* to name more than one.

daisy - _____

candy - _____

7 – 8. Circle the adjective that describes each underlined noun.

She likes spicy chili.   The room smells fresh.

I spit out the sour milk.   The glue was sticky.

Lesson #124

1. Add *–er* to adjectives to **compare two people or things.**
    Add *–est* to **compare more than two people.**

    Choose the correct adjective.

    Sue's house is (smaller / smallest) than ours.

    She has the (smaller / smallest) house on the street.

2. Write the mark for "move over" or "indent."   _____

3. Choose *has* or *have* to finish each sentence.

    Our game (has / have) started already.

    Terry (has / have) crawled under the bed.

4. Underline the verb.

    Our class wrote a letter to the President.

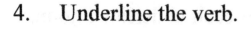

5.   Underline the correct sentence.

Emma and me wore the same dress.

Emma and I wore the same dress.

6.   Add "*s*" or "*–es*" to make the nouns name more than one.

catch - _____

tiger - _____

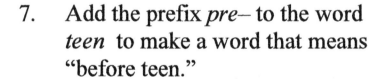

7.   Add the prefix *pre–* to the word *teen* to make a word that means "before teen."

pre- + teen ➡ _____

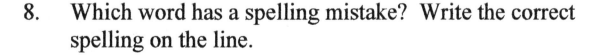

8.   Which word has a spelling mistake? Write the correct spelling on the line.

graet   would   next

_____

Lesson #125

1. Circle an antonym for the underlined word.

    Mrs. Crawley and Javier <u>worked</u> at the park all day.

    sang   played   painted   walked

2. Which part of the sentence is underlined?

    Rachel <u>lost her tooth</u>.

    naming part   action part

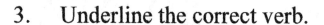

3. Underline the correct verb.

    The little boy (fly / flies) his kite.

    I (toss / tosses) the football.

4. List some names for a pet mouse.

    _____

    _____   _____

5.   Write a sentence about a pet mouse. Use one of the names
      from your list.

      _____

      _____

6.   Choose the correct adjective.

      The groundhog is (fatter / fattest) than my dog.

      It is the (fatter / fattest) animal I have ever seen.

7.   Underline the nouns in the sentence.

      A worm crawled up my leg.

8.   Write the verb from the sentence in #7.

      _____

Lesson #126

1.   Add the suffix –*ful* to the word *help* to make a word that means "full of help."

help + -ful ➡ _____

2.   **Homophones are words that sound alike but have different spellings and meanings.**

Example: <u>sale</u> and <u>sail</u>
I bought my coat on <u>sale</u>.
My dad bought a new <u>sail</u> for our boat.

Choose the correct homophone.

The wind (blue / blew) my hat off.

I (one / won) a prize.

4.   Write the mark for "add something."   _____

3.   Use the marks for "indent" and "add a period" to fix this sentence.

The band played loud music

5.   Write a proper noun for each word.

teacher - _____

street - _____

state - _____

6 – 7.   Use an adjective from the Word Box to finish each
sentence.

| yellow | hot | cold | tired |

We ate _____ soup for lunch.

I also had a glass of _____ milk.

For dessert, I had a _____ banana.

8.   Circle the correct verb.

Sammy (is / are) my best friend.

I (is / am) friends with Ronald, too.

Lesson #127

1. **Homophones** are words that **sound alike** but have **different spellings and meanings.**

    Choose the correct homophone.

    I need to change my (close / clothes).

    Mom needed (flower / flour) to make the cake.

2. Underline the correct verb.

    Last week the boys (play / played) baseball.

    Yesterday, grandpa (grill / grilled) hotdogs.

3. Replace the underlined words with a contraction.

    She <u>is not</u> going sledding.

    _____

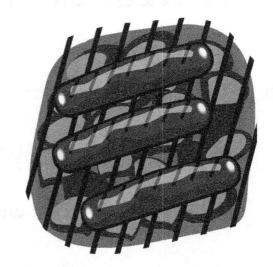

4 – 7. Write 3 or 4 sentences telling what you'd like to be when you grow up. Read it over and fix any mistakes using the special marks.

_____

_____

_____

_____

_____

8.   Drop the *e* before adding *–ing* to each word.

joke +-ing ➡ _____

dive +-ing ➡ _____

Lesson #128

1.   Circle the word that means almost the same as the underlined word.

My mom was very <u>mad</u> at my brother.

    happy   scream   angry

2.   Choose the correct verb.

The squirrel (has / have) buried some nuts.

The birds (has / have) made a nest in a tree.

3.   Circle the adjective that describes the underlined word.

I put a soft <u>blanket</u> on the bed.

Mom had on a silky <u>scarf</u>.

4.   Write the two words that make up the compound word.

lighthouse ➡ _____ + _____

5. Choose the correct homophone.

    I (hear / here) a train coming.

6. Add the suffix *–less* to the word *spot* to make a word that
    means "without a spot."

    spot + -less ➡ _____

7. Use a pronoun to replace the underlined words.

    <u>Army ants</u> can live in the rainforest. _____

    <u>Eliza</u> had to go to bed early. _____

8. Write the two words that make up each
    contraction.

    can't ➡ _____ _____

    don't ➡ _____ _____

Lesson #129

1. Choose the correct homophone.

    I want to (by / buy) peanuts at the game.

    I asked to sit (by / buy) the window.

2. **When you write, show what someone says by using quotation marks (" ") at the beginning and the end of what they say.**

    Example: Juan said, "Where are we going?"

    Read each sentence. Look for the exact words someone says. Put quotation marks before and after what they say.

    Sara said, I can't wait to go to the fair!

    Billy asked, Can I watch TV?

3. Circle the words with a short vowel sound.

    lost   lake   try   happy   big

4. Write the mark for "make capital." 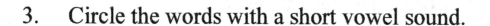 _____

5. Underline the naming part of the sentence.

    Amanda had to feed the chickens.

6. Choose the correct verb.

    The dog has (ran / run) after Louis.

    The birds have (came / come) back for the summer.

7. Which word has a spelling mistake? Write it correctly.

    behind   cryed   laugh

    _____

8. Write this sentence correctly.

    mr. Richards is∧ piano teacher⊙
    ‗   my

    _____

Lesson #130

1.   Choose the correct verb.

   Jen (see / saw) a raccoon in the woods.

   She has (saw / seen) them in the yard, too.

2.   Look for the exact words someone says. Put quotation marks before and after what they say.

   Ruby said, I'll take some pie.

   Javier asked, May I have a piece too?

3.   Which word means the opposite of the word *early*?

   early 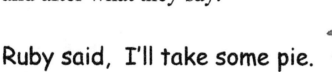   end   late   soon

4.   Use a contraction to take the place of the underlined words.

   Yang <u>is not</u> from this country.

   _____

5 – 6. Read the sentences below. Find 4 mistakes. Use the
        special marks to show how to fix the sentences.

I love to go to the zoo   my favorite animal is

the Monkey. The monkeys climb trees. i can't wait

to go the zoo!

7.   Write the sentence that has no
     mistake in #5 – 6.

_____

_____

_____

8.   Circle the correct adjective.

Your fish is (bigger / biggest) than mine.

My friend has the (nicer / nicest) house on the
block.

Lesson #131

1. Underline the correct sentence.

    I and Jesse played in the rain.

    Jesse and I played in the rain.

2. Fill in the correct end mark.

    The children made popcorn___

    Did you put butter on it___

    I love popcorn___

3. Which word rhymes with *fight*?

    fire   light   blind

4. Use an *apostrophe + –s* to show ownership.

    The hat belongs to Mr. Chen. It is Mr. Chen___ hat.

5.   Circle the adjective that describes each underlined word.

Erica opened her red <u>umbrella</u>.

Lisa waved to four <u>friends</u>.

Pablo ate a juicy <u>orange</u>.

6 – 8. Write three sentences comparing these two apes. Use
comparing words ending in –er or –est.

Koko

Benja

_____

_____

_____

_____

Lesson #132

1. Choose the correct homophone.

    She knew the (right / write) answer.

    Ty forgot to (right / write) his name
    on the paper.

2. Underline the verb in the action part
    of the sentence.

    The firefighters sprayed water

    on the flames.

3. Write the naming part of the sentence in #2.

    _____

4. Add "s" or "–es" to make these nouns name more than one.

    ash___   color___   brush___   read___

5 – 6. **When you use quotation marks around what someone says:**

   a) Always put a **comma after** words like *said* and *asked*.

   b) Begin the **first word inside** the quotation marks with a **capital letter**.

   c) Put the **end mark inside the quotation marks**.

   Use the rules above to fix these sentences.

A) Monica said   "Pizza is my favorite food."

B) Jake asked,   "when are we going hiking?"

C) My dad said, "I want to watch the news".

7.   Add the suffix *–less* to the word *shoe* to make a word that means "without shoes."

shoe + -less ➡ 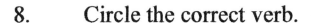 _____

8.   Circle the correct verb.

She (is / are) my boss.

We (am / are) good friends.

Lesson #133

1. **When you use quotation marks around what someone says:**

   - Always put a **comma after** words like *said* and *asked*.

   - Begin the **first word inside** the quotation marks with a **capital letter**.

   - Put the **end mark inside the quotation marks**.

   Use the rules above to fix these sentences.

   The woman asked   "Can you read this"?

   Ming said,   my favorite subject is art.

2. Choose the correct verb.

   She (help / helped) her mom set the table.

   She (has / have) helped her cook.

3. Write the two words that make up the compound word below.

   seaweed ➡ _____ + _____
   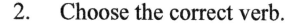

4. Write the mark that means "indent."   _____

5.   Use a pronoun in place of the underlined words.

<u>The bike</u> is green.   _____

<u>Meg and Fran</u> ran in the relay race.   _____

6.   Underline the words that should
      begin with a capital letter.

christmas   september

school   ohio

7.   **When you write the title of a book, begin the first word
      of every important word in the title with a capital letter.
      Draw a line under the title.**

      Example: <u>Charlotte's Web</u>   <u>Ira Sleeps Over</u>

      Underline each title. Use the mark for "make capital" to
      show which words should be capitalized in these titles.

      pirate girl   queen bee

8.   Write the mark that means
      "make lower case."   _____

Lesson #134

1.   Choose the correct homophone.

     We went to (our / hour) family picnic.

     It took us an (our / hour) to get ready.

2.   Underline the book titles below.

     Night Dancer   Harry Potter

3.   Underline the action part of the sentence.

     We drove my dad to the airport.

4.   Put in a comma after the word *said* or *asked* and put quotation marks around what the person said.

     My teacher asked   Has anyone ever seen a shark?

     Jon said   I saw one when we went to Florida.

5.   Add the prefix *re–* to the word *say* to make a word that means "to say again."

re- + say ➡ _____

6 – 7.   Put the nouns in the Word Box in the correct category.

car	candy	school	doctor	baby
store	book	park	boy	pencil

People	Places	Things

8.   Underline the verb.

The kitten slept in a basket.

Lesson #135

1. Replace the underlined words with a contraction.

    Some animals <u>do not</u> eat meat.   _____

    Patrick <u>is not</u> home. _____

2. Underline the book titles.

    Superfudge

    Molly Goes to France

3. Choose the correct verb.

    I (hit / hits) the ball and run to the base.

    Keith (catch / catches) the ball and throws me out.

4. Circle the adjective that describes the underlined word.

    The <u>toast</u> smelled burnt.

    The puppy had a wet <u>nose</u>.

5.   Use the mark for "make capital" and "take something out" to
      fix this sentence.

      We don't have school on the thanksgiving.

6.   Underline the action part of the sentence.

      We watched a puppet show.

7.   Underline the sentence.

      Dug a hole.

      The flowers smell sweet.

      The garden.

8.   Write your own sentence about flowers.

_____

_____

_____

Lesson #136

1. Fill in a word to describe each word below. The word can describe how something looks, feels, smells, or tastes.

    _____ giraffe   _____ honey

2. Choose the correct homophone.

    (To / Two) bats flew by me.

    I ran home (to / two) tell my mom.

3. Underline the proper nouns.

    Austin went to Washington with Grandpa.

4. Add an *apostrophe* after the *–s* to show ownership of these nouns that name more than one.

    classes__ books

    kittens__ basket

5.   Put quotation marks around what each person is saying.
      Make sure to put a comma after the word *said* or *asked.*

Mom asked   What kind of books do you like?

Leah said   I love picture books.

6.   Write the two words that make
      up this compound word.

sunglasses ➡ _____ + _____

7.   Underline two *antonyms* or words that mean the opposite.

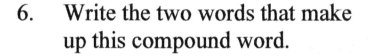

     quiet   clean   long   dirty

8.   Choose the correct verb.

Hoshi (finish / finishes) first.

Uncle Norman (fix / fixes) the clock.

Lesson #137

1. Which part of the sentence is underlined?

   <u>Mrs. Cabot</u> is our babysitter.

   action part   naming part

2. Underline the book titles in this sentence.

   Two of my favorite books are

   Curious George and Stellaluna.

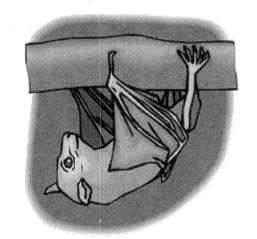

3. Replace each underlined word
   with a pronoun.

   <u>Tina</u> rang the doorbell.   _____

   <u>Mark</u> opened the door.   _____

4. Which word is a *synonym* for (means almost the same as) the
   word *jump*?

   jump ➡   run   laugh   leap

5. Put quotation marks around what each person says.

My teacher asked, Who discovered America?

Ivanna answered, Christopher Columbus discovered

America.

6. Underline the nouns that name people.

My brother is a carpenter.

7. Write 4 adjectives to describe yourself.

Example: funny, pretty, smart

_____   _____

_____   _____

8. Choose the correct verb.

Kevin (was / were) the leader yesterday.

Lesson #138

1. Replace the underlined words with a contraction. (Use the Help Pages if you need to.)

   I <u>cannot</u> tell what is in the box. _____

   I <u>do not</u> want to open it until later. _____

2. Circle the adjective that describes the underlined word.

   Grandma found her round <u>glasses</u>.

   Ray's yellow <u>bucket</u> is full of sand.

3. Which word has a spelling mistake? Write the correct spelling on the line.

   heard   nothing   lauf

   _____

4. Write the mark for "add a period." _____

5.   Underline the book title.

Lily read Ramona the Pest last summer.

6.   Fill in the correct end mark.

What a surprise___

Stand up straight___

She found a quarter on the floor___

7 – 8.   Read the sentences. Find four mistakes and show how to
          fix the mistakes using the special marks.

My cousin and I love to go to the playground on

saturdays. There are so many things do. It is so

close to our our house. Our Parents never worry

about us while we're there.

Lesson #139

1 – 3. Draw a picture of a person, a place, and a thing. Write a
        sentence using each noun.

Person	Place	Thing

A) _____

B) _____

C) _____

4. Change the *y* to *i* before adding *–es*.

daisy ➡ _____

5.   Underline the correct sentence.

i will be in third grade next year.

My brother and I are twins.

6.   Choose the correct homophone.

I ate a (pair / pear) for lunch.

Mom bought me a new (pear / pair) of shoes.

7.   Add the prefix *un–* to the word *necessary* to make a word
      that means "not necessary."

un- + necessary ➡ _____

8.   Choose the correct adjective.

Jack is (stronger / strongest) than Dave.

Manny is the (stronger / strongest) in
the class.

Lesson #140

1. Use the marks for "make capital" and "add a period" to fix this sentence.

   reggie raced his horse in the derby on sunday

2. The **naming part of a sentence** is also called the **subject**.

   Underline the subject of the sentence.

   The children cleaned up the playground.

3. Underline the nouns that name things in this sentence.

   The bird flapped its wings.

4. Write the group of words that makes a complete thought.

   Lost my keys. We searched for them.

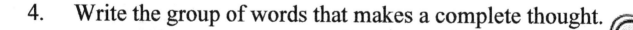

   _____

   _____

5.   Add an *apostrophe* + *–s* to each single noun to show ownership.

      The leash belongs to the dog. It is the dog___ leash.

6.   Use a pronoun to take the place of the underlined words. (Use *he, she, it, we,* or *they.*)

      The <u>workers</u> ate their lunch.   _____

      The <u>chair</u> had a broken leg.   _____

7.   Choose the correct homophone.

      We took a (plane / plain) to Florida.

      We drew the picture on (plane / plain) paper.

8.   Which words have the same vowel sound?

      tray   rock   bake   run   rake

Simple Solutions

English Grammar & Writing Mechanics

level 2

Help Pages

Help Pages

Kinds of Sentences:		
Statement	tells something	.
Question	asks something	?
Command	tells someone to do something	.
Exclamation	shows emotion	!

Editing Marks:	
Capital letter	≡
End Punctuation	⊙ ⊕ ⊘
Add Something	∧
Change to lower case	/
Take something out	ℐ
Indent	¶

Helping Verbs:
have
has

Steps in the Writing Process:		
1.	Prewriting	getting ideas for writing
2.	Drafting	putting your ideas into writing
3.	Revising	adding or taking out to make your writing better
4.	Editing	using editing marks to correct mistakes
5.	Publishing	sharing your writing with others

Help Pages

Rules for Spelling:
1. Words ending in *s, x, z, ch,* or *sh,* add *–es* to make the plural.
2. To make compound words, usually join two words without changing the spelling of either word.
3. When adding a suffix to a word, the spelling of the word sometimes changes; the suffix does not usually change.
4. When a word ends in a consonant plus *y,* change the *y* to *i* and add *–es.*
5. If a word ends in *–e* and you want to add a suffix that begins with a vowel, drop the *–e* before adding the suffix.

Subject Pronouns:

Singular	I, you, he, she, it
Plural	we, you, they

Prefixes:

un- means "not"
re- means "again"
pre- means "before"

Contractions:

cannot	can't
do not	don't
does not	doesn't
is not	isn't

Suffixes:

-er means "someone who does something"
-ful means "full of"
-less means "without"

Help Pages

Vocabulary:		
Sentence		a group of words that tells a complete thought
Naming / Subject		tells who or what the sentence is about
Action/Predicate		tells what the subject does or is
Synonym		a word that means the same or almost the same as another word
Antonym		a word that means the opposite of another word
Homophone		words that sound alike but have different spellings and meanings

Parts of Speech:	
Noun	a word that names a person, place, or thing
Verb	a word that shows action or a state of being; a verb is the main word in the action part of the sentence
Pronoun	a word that takes the place of a noun
Adjective	a word that describes a noun

Rules for Using Capital Letters:	
The beginning of every sentence.	Names of Special People, Places, or Things
Everytime you use "I"	Important Words in a Book Title
Days of the Week	
Months of the Year	Titles of People
Holidays	

Help Pages

Verb Tenses:	
Present Time Verbs	Most present time verbs end in –*s* when the subject is singular. (run runs)
Past Time Verbs	Verbs that tell an action that has already happened usually add –*ed* to show past time.

Irregular Verbs:		
Present	**Past**	**With *has* or *have***
come	came	*has or have* come
do	did	*has or have* done
give	gave	*has or have* given
go	went	*has or have* gone
run	ran	*has or have* run
see	saw	*has or have* seen

Rules for Showing Ownership:	
Single Noun	Add an apostrophe + -s
Noun that names more than one	Add an apostrophe after the –s

Rules for Using Quotation Marks:
- Use quotation marks (" ") around what someone says.
- Always put a comma after words like <u>said</u> and <u>asked</u>.
- The first word inside the quotation marks has a capital letter.
- Put the end mark inside the quotation marks.